—African-American Biographies—

IDA B.
WELLS-BARNETT

Crusader Against Lynching

Series Consultant:
Dr. Russell L. Adams, Chairman
Department of Afro-American Studies, Howard University

Elaine Slivinski Lisandrelli

Enslow Publishers, Inc.

44 Fadem Road	PO Box 38
Box 699	Aldershot
Springfield, NJ 07081	Hants GU12 6BP
USA	UK

> *In memory of Norma DeNault Grula*
> *(June 20, 1926–May 27, 1996)*

Library of Congress Cataloging-in-Publication Data

Lisandrelli, Elaine Slivinski
    Ida B. Wells-Barnett : crusader against lynching / Elaine
Slivinski Lisandrelli.
        p. cm. — (African-American biographies)
    Includes bibliographical references and index.
    Summary: Traces the life and career of the African-American
journalist and social activist who spoke out against the lynching
of blacks in the South.
    ISBN 0-89490-947-9
    1. Wells-Barnett, Ida B., 1862–1931—Juvenile literature. 2. Afro-American
women civil rights workers—Biography—Juvenile literature.
3. Afro-American women journalists—Biography—Juvenile literature.
4. Afro-Americans—Crimes against—Juvenile literature. 5. Lynching—United
States—History—Juvenile literature. 6. United States—Race relations—Juvenile
literature. [1. Wells-Barnett, Ida B., 1862–1931. 2. Afro-American women civil
rights workers. 3. Afro-American women journalists. 4. Civil rights workers.
5. Journalists. 6. Afro-Americans—Biography. 7. Women—Biography.] I. Title.
II. Series.
E185.97.W55L57 1998
323'.092—dc21
[B]   97-34253
                                                CIP
                                                AC

Printed in the United States of America

10 9 8 7 6 5 4 3 2 1

Illustration Credits: Arkansas History Commission, p. 108; Department of Special
Collections, the University of Chicago Library, pp. 4, 33, 47, 61, 67, 83, 91, 95, 98, 101,
105, 112; Marshall County Historical Museum, Holly Springs, Mississippi, pp. 15, 17,
21, 23; Minor B. Wade, Gillman Paper Company Collection, p. 40 [the publisher would
like to thank the NAACP for its advice about this photograph]; National Archives, Still
Picture Branch, pp. 55, 64; Special Collections and Archives, W.E.B. Du Bois Library,
University of Massachusetts Amherst, p. 78.

Cover Illustration: Department of Special Collections, the University of Chicago Library

The publisher gratefully acknowledges permission for the following:

Excerpts from *CRUSADE FOR JUSTICE: THE AUTOBIOGRAPHY OF IDA B. WELLS*,
edited by Alfreda M. Duster (in the Negro American Biographies and Autobiographies
series, editor John Hope Franklin), copyright © 1970 by the University of Chicago.
Reprinted by permission of the University of Chicago Press.

Excerpts from the Ida B. Wells papers. Used by permission of the Department of
Special Collections, the University of Chicago Library.

CONTENTS

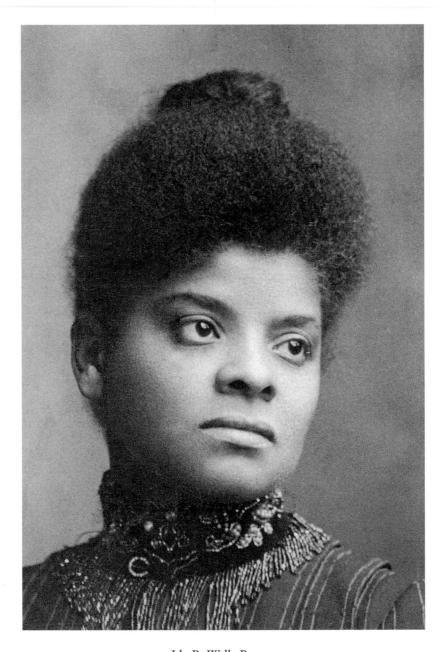

Ida B. Wells-Barnett

1

SPEAKING OUT AGAINST INJUSTICE

For twenty-one-year-old Ida B. Wells, one spring day in 1884 began like most workdays. She boarded the train in Memphis, Tennessee, for her ten-mile ride to Woodstock, where she taught elementary school. She sat down in the first-class car and opened the book she was reading. As the conductor approached her seat, Wells handed him her first-class ticket, just as she always did. But on this day, for some reason, the conductor handed the ticket back to her. That was surprising at first, even a bit jarring, but Wells put it out of her mind and returned to her reading. The train chugged along, and the conductor continued collecting tickets from other passengers. Little did Wells know that soon she would make her mark on history.

When the conductor returned, he told Wells she must move to a second-class car. "I refused," she said later. "The forward car was the smoker, and as I was in the ladies' car I proposed to stay. He tried to drag me out of the seat, but the moment he caught hold of my arm I fastened my teeth in the back of his hand."[1]

The conductor broke free and stormed off. But soon he was back, this time with two other men. The three men grabbed the four-foot-six-inch-tall Wells and dragged her from the first-class section. White passengers cheered and even stood on their seats to get a better view of the disturbance.

Wells described the difficult choice she had to make: "By this time the train had stopped at the first station. When I saw that they were determined to drag me into the smoker, which was already filled with colored people and those who were smoking, I said I would get off the train rather than go in—which I did."[2]

At the next stop, Wells got off the train, still clutching her ticket in her hand. She had not been hurt physically, but the sleeves of her linen duster had been torn out. Despite the humiliation, Wells did not let this incident get the best of her.

A year earlier, the Supreme Court had overturned

the Civil Rights Act of 1875, a law that prohibited racial discrimination in public places. By overturning this law, the Supreme Court allowed private individuals and organizations (like the railroad) to set up separate accommodations for blacks and whites. On the train from Memphis, Ida B. Wells had experienced firsthand the bitter taste of segregation. Many African Americans put up with the system of separate railroad cars for whites and for blacks, but Ida B. Wells did not. She believed in equality, and she would not accept this unfair treatment.[3]

She hired Memphis's only black attorney, Thomas F. Cassels, to sue the Chesapeake, Ohio, and Southwestern Railroad Company for refusing to give her the first-class seat for which she had paid. It was a courageous act for a young African-American woman to challenge a powerful railroad. But her lawsuit did not go smoothly. She soon discovered that the railroad had paid off her attorney so he would not represent her well. Disappointed, but still determined, Wells hired another attorney, a former judge named James M. Greer.

Her new attorney worked hard, and in December of 1884, seven months after she was forced off the train, Wells won the lawsuit. Judge J. O. Pierce believed that the railroad did not offer Wells a seat on the train equal to the seats offered to white passengers. He ordered the railroad to pay the maximum fine of $300. Judge Pierce also ordered that Wells be awarded $500 in damages, since she had been forced from the first-class car. A Memphis paper printed the following uncomplimentary headline: A Darky Damsel Obtains a Verdict for Damages Against the Chesapeake and Ohio Railroad.[4]

Wells wrote her own account of her lawsuit for *The Living Way*, an African-American church newspaper. In the article she reminded readers that if they would just stand up for their rights, they would be able to keep them. Her account of her 1884 railroad suit in *The Living Way* marked her start in the field of journalism. Eventually, her writing appeared in other African-American newspapers nationwide. Her weekly columns encouraged self-help, education, and social reform.

The railroad appealed the case to a higher court. On April 11, 1887, two and a half years after her first victory, the Tennessee Supreme Court reversed the lower court's decision. This higher court now ruled against Wells in the railroad suit, on the grounds that the smoking car was equal to the first-class car.

In addition, the Tennessee Supreme Court said Wells was harassing the railroad. They ordered her to pay more than $200 in court costs—a great deal of money for a young African-American schoolteacher in 1887 struggling to pay her rent. But the financial loss was not the only problem. The pain of personal loss cut deep. Wells recorded her feelings:

I felt so disappointed because I had hoped such great things from my suit for my people generally. I have firmly believed all along that the law was on our side and would, when we appealed to it, give us justice. I feel shorn of that belief and utterly discouraged, and just now, if it were possible, would gather my race in my arms and fly away with them.[5]

Ida B. Wells would spend the rest of her life gathering her race in her arms. She became an important African-American journalist during a time when women, especially African-American women, were not encouraged to have careers. Her words became a powerful force against injustice. She did not always win her battles, but she did succeed in bringing attention to inequality.

Her deep concern for others and her ability to face challenges with courage and determination were lessons learned in her early days in Holly Springs, Mississippi.

2

BORN A SLAVE

Ida Bell Wells was born a slave in Holly Springs, Mississippi, on July 16, 1862, during the second year of the Civil War, the bitter conflict that divided the United States against itself.

Her parents, Jim and Lizzie Wells, had been born into slavery, too. Ida's mother, Lizzie (Elizabeth Warrenton), was taken from her family when she was only seven years old and sold to slave traders. Later she was sold again. This terrible practice of breaking up families was recounted by a former slave:

> Slaves was treated in most cases like cattle. A man went about the country buyin' up slaves like buyin' up cattle.

. . . Then he'd sell 'em to the highest bidder. Oh! it was pitiful to see children taken from their mothers' breasts, mothers sold, husbands sold from wives. One woman he was to buy had a baby, and of course the baby come before he bought her and he wouldn't buy the baby, said he hadn't bargained to buy the baby, too, and he just wouldn't.[1]

Ida often heard about the hard time her mother had as a slave and the many beatings she suffered at the hands of cruel masters. Ida also heard how her parents met. When Lizzie was a slave for Mr. Bolling, a prominent builder in Holly Springs, she fell in love with another slave, Jim Wells. They married and began to raise a family that eventually included eight children, one of whom died very young of spinal meningitis.

Born in Tippah County, Mississippi, on a plantation, Ida's father, Jim, was the son of Mr. Wells—his white master—and Peggy, a slave woman. At the time of slavery, it was not uncommon for white masters to father children with their black slaves.

Ida learned that her father was never whipped or auctioned off. Jim Wells's father/master made sure he learned a trade as a carpenter and had him apprenticed to Mr. Bolling. Although Jim Wells's life had not been as cruel as life was for many other slaves, a terrible injustice remained with him always: One day he had to watch his mother being stripped of her clothing and forced to stand naked as a rawhide whip cut deep into her flesh.

This terrible act had been ordered by Polly Wells, the white wife of Mr. Wells, the very day after her husband—Jim's father—had died. Years later, Ida longed to know more of this humiliating incident but felt uncomfortable asking any more questions about the tragic scene.[2]

After the Civil War ended in 1865, the country had to be made whole again. It needed to heal—to recover and become a stronger nation. In the South this period was called Reconstruction. At the beginning of Reconstruction there were problems to overcome, but for many it was also a time of promise and hope.

As part of this new era, former slaves were allowed to renew their wedding vows. During slavery, African Americans had to get permission from their masters to marry. Although slaves could not legally become husband and wife, many couples were seen as married. They did not have fancy ceremonies, and sometimes a short Scripture reading was given. The couple usually held hands and jumped across a broomstick. The next morning they had to be ready to work for the master again.

When freedom came, Ida's parents, who had both lived in slavery until the end of the war, decided to be married again. This social choice revealed the strong commitment Lizzie and Jim had to each other and to their children. Jim and Lizzie continued working for Mr. Bolling, this time for pay. Lizzie created delicious meals as Bolling's cook, and Jim used his expert skills as a carpenter.

Jim Wells also took an interest in the politics of the time and was concerned about protecting newfound freedoms. About two years after the Civil War ended, African-American men were allowed to vote in Mississippi elections. Mr. Bolling tried to influence Jim Wells to vote for the Democratic Party, the party at that time led by former slave owners. Strong-willed Jim voted instead for the Republicans—the party of President Abraham Lincoln and emancipation—the party at that time that offered the most hope for former slaves. As a result, Bolling fired Jim Wells. Without regret, Jim Wells moved his family and started his own business.[3]

At the end of the Civil War, 90 percent of African Americans in the South were illiterate. For nearly a century it had been considered a crime in most southern states to teach African Americans, slave or free, to read or write. A few white people who were caught doing so were slapped with fines and jail sentences. Some blacks who were caught were beaten or had their thumbs or toes cut off. Many whites feared the power the written word would give the slave, but blacks recognized the magic written words could perform—a magic that opened up whole new worlds.

Students and teachers stand outside one of the first schools for African Americans in Holly Springs, Mississippi.

As new public schools opened throughout the South, many African Americans could at last satisfy their passion for learning. They saw education as the main hope for their children's future. Lizzie Wells, hungry for an education for her children and herself, even went to school with her children until she learned to read her beloved Bible. Lizzie also used her newly discovered writing skills to track down long-lost kin through letters. Like many former slaves who had been torn away from family members and sold, Lizzie was unsuccessful in reuniting the family of her youth.

Jim and Lizzie Wells had high expectations for their children, and Ida knew these expectations well: "Our job was to go to school and learn all we could," she wrote.[4] Ida attended Shaw University (later named Rust College), a school for former slaves, until she was sixteen years old. Although it was called a university, it offered instruction at all grades and levels for African Americans. Ida completed her assignments, read for hours by the light of a kerosene lantern, and thirsted to learn more.

Ida grew up during the period of Reconstruction, with the South experiencing violent change. Mississippi was torn by struggles between blacks and whites. Often Jim Wells asked Ida to read the newspaper to him and his friends. Ida read articles filled with painful words: words revealing that whites did not want their children attending classes with blacks; words blaming African

This African-American family lived in Holly Springs during the time of Ida B. Wells's youth.

Americans for the bad economy in the South; and words preaching the untruth that African Americans were genetically inferior. Ida also read about the brutal murders of African-American leaders.

Despite the problems that existed between the races, many African Americans still felt that there was hope for a better life. Ida's family and friends believed that they, too, would share in the benefits of freedom.

Ida also learned hope and compassion in her home. On Sundays the Wells family made time for church and Bible reading. They were proud of winning a prize for best family attendance at Sunday school. The children were taught to help one another and do chores. Ida changed diapers and gave Saturday night baths to the younger children. She looked out for her sister Eugenia, who had become paralyzed in the lower part of her body and could not walk. Ida scrubbed wooden floors and hung clothes to dry in the spring breezes scented with magnolia. She chopped vegetables for her mother's favorite recipes and cleaned up after family suppers filled with good food and laughter. When work was done, there was time for old-fashioned games and family stories.

Unfortunately, tragedy would soon strike this happy home, and Ida would have to face one of her first major challenges.

3

YELLOW FEVER

During the hot, humid months of July and August 1878, the dreaded yellow fever whirled through southern towns, bringing great suffering. People who woke up with headaches, chills, or fever often died within a week. In some communities, two to three hundred—men, women, and children alike—died on a single day. Nothing could stop this tragedy. Soon the dreaded yellow jack, as some people called it, invaded Holly Springs, Mississippi, the small hometown of sixteen-year-old Ida B. Wells. Fortunately for Ida, she was not at home when the fever struck.

Ida was miles away on her Grandma Peggy's farm,

where corn and cotton grew plentifully. Ida spent time preparing mash to fatten the hogs for fall market and listening to her grandparents' stories of slavery and dreams of freedom. Ida assumed that her father had taken her mother, three brothers, and three sisters out of the infected area to a safe country place.[1] Since mail delivery was so irregular, she did not expect to hear from them.

But the Wells family had not left Holly Springs as thousands of other residents had done, their wagons piled high with beds, trunks, and small furniture. Unknown to Ida, her parents, Jim and Lizzie Wells, stayed in Holly Springs, caring for the sick and offering comfort to people yellowed with jaundice and bleeding internally. Her father, a skilled carpenter, made coffins for those who did not survive the horrible epidemic.

One late summer day, several friends of the Wells family arrived at Ida's grandmother's farm and sadly handed Ida a letter: "Jim and Lizzy Wells have both died of the fever. They died within twenty-four hours of each other. . . . The children are all at home. . . . Send word to Ida."[2]

Sadness filled the farmhouse. Although many advised her against going into the infected town, Ida's devotion to her brothers and sisters won out. Ida wanted to rush back to Holly Springs, but because no passenger trains would even venture into

People try to leave town during the yellow fever epidemic of 1878.

the disease-ridden area, she rode home in the caboose of a freight train.

Ida arrived home to find two of the Wells children in bed with chills. She prayed for their recovery. She received the sad news that her nine-month-old baby brother Stanley had also died of the fever. Ida's return was a special comfort to her sister Eugenia.

Holly Springs was a picture of death, just like the two hundred other areas in the South where the disease had struck. The air was heavy with the stench of decomposition and disinfectants and the smoke of burning clothes, mattresses, and bedding. The mournful knell of the church bells, ringing for lives lost, was heard too often. Even rats had died from eating the flesh of some dead bodies that had not been buried. Fortunately, after the first frost blanketed the town, the yellow fever epidemic ended.

Ida's father, Jim Wells, had been a leader in the brotherhood of Prince Hall Masons, a national group that did charitable work. Now his Masonic brothers, assuming the role of protectors, made a plan for the newly orphaned children. Four separate homes awaited Annie, Lily, James, and George. Since no one offered Eugenia a home, she would be sent to a poorhouse. The Masons agreed that Ida was old enough to fend for herself.

When Ida learned of their plan, she refused to let it happen. She had been silent but could hold back no

Gravediggers prepare mass graves to bury those who had died of yellow fever.

longer. Ida insisted that her parents would "turn over in their graves" if they knew that their children were being scattered in so many different directions.[3]

Some of the Masons laughed at Ida's suggestion that she could take care of the family. It would not be the last time in her life Ida would be laughed at. She stood firm: Her brothers and sisters would not be divided up. She would raise them together in the home their father had left them.

After realizing Ida was determined to have her way, some of the Masons gave in and advised her to get a teaching job. It pained her to give up her chance of completing school, but she made the sacrifice. She lied about her age, lengthened her skirts to appear older, passed a special examination, and became a country schoolteacher. She earned twenty-five dollars a month teaching in a one-room schoolhouse. She had free time only for reading, a pastime she loved and one that helped her forget her troubles.

The teenage Ida B. Wells journeyed the six miles home at the end of the schoolweek riding on the back of a mule, carrying the eggs and butter the country folk had been kind enough to give her. She was welcomed by her mother's friend, who cared for the children during the week, after Ida's grandmother became too ill to take care of them any longer.

On Saturdays and Sundays, Ida washed, ironed, cooked, and cleaned for her brothers and sisters. On

Sunday afternoon she began the mule ride back to the country school. It was not an easy task for a sixteen-year-old girl to work all week teaching school, live with families of her students, and return home on weekends to try to be a mother and father to her younger brothers and sisters.

Even though Ida B. Wells wanted to keep her family together, it became harder and harder. After a few years, Ida's Aunt Fannie, her father's sister who lived in Memphis, Tennessee, offered to help. Fannie had lost her own husband to the yellow jack. Although Fannie had three children of her own to raise, she now invited Ida to come to Memphis.

Ida worked on making new arrangements. She had to separate the children, but this time she was able to have relatives care for them. Ida's Aunt Belle, her mother's sister, was able to take care of Eugenia, and James and George worked on Aunt Belle's farm. Annie and Lily, the two youngest, traveled with Ida to Memphis to live with Aunt Fannie.

Memphis, a city much larger than Holly Springs, offered more opportunity for Ida. It also presented unexpected challenges.

4

MEMPHIS

emphis had much more for Ida B. Wells to see and do than Holly Springs had. She walked the cobblestone streets and loved to shop in the many department stores, often buying a stylish hat to accent her upswept hairstyle or a parasol to accessorize one of her fine dresses.

She enjoyed Memphis, a major river town of the Mississippi Delta. At the time Wells lived there, the city was thriving even though it had recently experienced war, military occupation, and defeat and had suffered through three yellow fever epidemics. It boasted ten railroads and three hundred factories and was a major market for cotton, hardwood, and wholesale groceries.

Steamboats and cotton barges could be seen on the waterfront. Churches and synagogues lined the streets. About 40 percent of the population was African American, and some met with success establishing businesses in Memphis.

Wells loved attending plays and enjoyed William Shakespeare's *Hamlet* amid the glow of gaslights in one of the Memphis theaters. Although she was not interested in marriage at the time, Wells liked the companionship of male friends who escorted her to church, social events, and concerts. She spent hours talking to them and was not afraid to beat them in a game of Parcheesi or checkers. She enjoyed exchanging cards, letters, and photographs with them.

Wells taught a Sunday school class for young African-American men and hoped to have a positive influence on them.[1] She became a member of the Lyceum, a Memphis literary club that met every Friday afternoon at Lemoyne Normal Institute. Wells and other members recited essays, poems, and excerpts from plays. They held debates and book discussions, and they listened to music. The meetings ended with the reading of *The Evening Star*, the club's newsletter, which Wells edited.

About the time her lawsuit against the railroad had first gone to court, when she was teaching in Woodstock, Wells had passed a qualifying exam to teach in the Memphis city schools. She became one of only about twenty African-American public-school teachers in Memphis. She earned nearly sixty dollars a month teaching. Most African-American women in Memphis worked as housekeepers or did laundry for as little as sixteen dollars a month.

Although her employment opportunities were better than those for most other African-American women, her working conditions were inferior to the working conditions of white teachers at the time. Salaries of black teachers and principals were lower than those of whites. Black teachers had larger classes than many of the white teachers.

Wells tried to save money, but it was often difficult after paying for rent, carfare, clothing, lessons, and attorney's fees. The school board often paid the teachers two to three months late. When her salary finally came, Wells usually had to use all the money to pay off some loans or bills for items she had already bought on credit. She had a weakness for nice clothing even when she could not afford it. One time she spent almost half a month's salary on a dress: $15.80 for material and $7.60 for the labor of a seamstress.

During Wells's early teaching days in Woodstock and Memphis, Aunt Fannie had taken care of Annie and Lily. Ida found it comforting to have them nearby to share some of her joys and sorrows, but in 1885 things changed. Lured by the promise of good work, better pay, and a healthier climate, Aunt Fannie moved to California. She took Annie and Lily and her own three children to discover a better life in Visalia, a town two hundred miles south of San Francisco. Wells remained in Memphis.

That same year, Wells began what became known as her *Memphis Diary*. In the notebook she wrote five or six entries each month. In her entries, which were usually about three to five pages long, she often used a first initial to refer to a friend or relative.

Many pages of her diary record times when Wells felt sad and lonely.[2] Her writings reveal a young woman who was often swayed by emotions and sometimes had trouble making a decision. She worked hard at controlling her temper, and she wanted to improve her relationships with others, "Father help me, I pray be more thoughtful & and considerate in speech, and in action be consistent," she wrote.[3]

She felt guilty enjoying herself when she knew Aunt Fannie had Lily and Annie to provide for.[4] Even though money was tight, Wells often sent ten dollars a month support for her two sisters. Sometimes she made dresses for Annie and Lily.

At the time she began her diary, Ida's brother James was nineteen and George was sixteen. She consoled them through their job difficulties and urged them to stay away from drinking, gambling, and friends that had a bad influence on them. She wished she had more patience with them, especially James: "I can get along well enough with other boys [her students] but am too hasty and impatient with my own."[5]

Wells's good friend Alfred Froman, an older gentleman who owned a harness and saddle shop in Memphis, helped her look out for her brothers. It had been many years since Wells's father had died, and she often called Froman "Dad" or "Pap."

The summer of 1886, when Wells turned twenty-four years old, was an adventurous time for her. She traveled by train through Missouri, Kansas, Colorado, Utah, and California. Her travel experiences became the subjects of newspaper articles that appeared in *The Watchman, The Gate City Press,* and the *A.M.E. Church Review.* She delighted in meeting African Americans who had earned important positions, including a school principal from Indiana, the Kansas state auditor, a candidate for the Colorado State Legislature, and the editor of San Francisco's major black newspaper. She went to a meeting of the National Education Association in Topeka, Kansas, where one talk was titled "The Problem of Race Education in the United States."

She spent a month and a half with Aunt Fannie in Visalia. Although she was happy to see her sisters, she was disappointed by the small town and its segregated school.[6] Wells taught in Visalia's one-room school for four days, but it angered her that in Visalia, African Americans had chosen to have a separate school for their children.[7] She felt a sense of duty to her aunt, but could not support this segregated school. Good-byes were especially difficult since Annie refused to leave Aunt Fannie and her cousin Ida (Aunt Fannie's daughter was named after Ida B. Wells). Wells remembered the struggle: "I realized it would be much easier for me to manage with one instead of two half-grown girls on my hands. So after a promise from my aunt that she would care for Annie as if she were her own daughter, I agreed to leave her there."[8]

Back in Memphis, Wells waited for additional word about her lawsuit against the railroad, handled a full-time teaching job, wrote articles for newspapers, and cared for her sister Lily. She tried to be mother and father to Lily. She made Lily skirts and dresses, bought her shoes and books, and provided her with love and understanding. Rumors spread that Lily was Wells's illegitimate daughter instead of her sister. Wells ignored the rumors.

During this period when Wells was in her early and mid-twenties, she built the foundation of her career as a journalist. In her diaries she often jotted down notes for future articles. At a time when the white press hardly ever reported news about black people, Wells felt the need to inform her people about national issues and local events. Wells used the pen name "Iola" and was happy that the newspaper gave her space. "The correspondence I had built up in newspaper work gave me

This copy of an engraved portrait of Ida B. Wells appeared in an African-American newspaper in the early days of her journalistic career.

an outlet through which to express the real 'me' and I enjoyed my work to the utmost."[9]

While attending the newly established Fisk University in Nashville, Tennessee, during the summer months, Wells wrote for the student newspaper. This experience led to a part-time job as editor of *The Evening Star*, a church-related newspaper, and then to the editorship of another church newspaper, *The Living Way*. In 1889 Wells became a partner in the *Free Speech and Headlight*, later known as the *Free Speech*, a small Baptist weekly in Memphis.

She was grateful for the support of African-American journalist William J. Simmons, editor of the *American Baptist*, a publication of the American Baptist Home Missionary Society. Simmons admired Wells's work and was the first person to pay her for her writing. She always remembered the encouragement he gave her and the new worlds he opened up for her. When she represented his paper at a press conference in Washington, D.C., she was elected secretary of the National Press Association. It was at this convention that she first saw Frederick Douglass, the great African-American leader. Douglass was a former slave who had taught himself to read and write and who used his eloquent voice to speak out against racial injustice. Their paths would cross again in future days.

Wells felt strongly that African Americans who had earned an education and achieved success had a social responsibility to those of the race who were less fortunate.[10] She attended meetings of local civil rights groups and spoke out against the social, political, economic, and racial difficulties facing fellow African Americans in the 1880s.

Wells could not help but write an editorial protesting the separate and unequal conditions in the black schools. It troubled her that only half of the African-American school-age children attended school. She resented the fact that those children who did go to school were in run-down buildings and overcrowded classrooms and had very few books to read. She questioned the motives of school board members who hired unqualified teachers.[11] The editorial cost Wells her teaching job: "I had rather feared that might be the result; but I had taken a chance in the interest of the children of our race and had lost out."[12]

The lack of support shown by the parents of the African-American students saddened her. When she heard comments like "Miss Ida, you ought not to have done it, you might have known they would fire you," she realized that she would not always have the encouragement of her race.[13] But that knowledge did not deter her from taking stands on issues she strongly believed in. She later wrote, "But I thought it was right to strike a blow against a glaring evil and I did not regret it."[14]

Ida B. Wells showed signs of leadership in a time

when most of the African-American leaders were males. As the last decade of the nineteenth century began, segregation became more common and violence toward African Americans increased.

This young crusader, who had experienced some of this hatred firsthand and had fought back through the legal system, was about to encounter an experience that would outrage her even more than the humiliation she had felt when she was denied her rights on the train.

5

LYNCHING

da B. Wells had been proud when her good friend Thomas Moss opened the People's Grocery Company just outside Memphis. Moss and his buddies Calvin McDowell and William Stewart chose to become businessmen at a difficult time when blacks were starting to gain power and whites did not want to share it.[1] Their store did well, and their success angered W. H. Barrett, the white man who owned and operated a grocery store across the street from them. Resenting his new competition, Barrett threatened to ruin their business.[2] He spread a rumor that a white mob was going to trash their store. Moss, McDowell, and Stewart prepared for trouble.

On Saturday, March 5, 1892, nine gun-carrying whites descended upon the People's Grocery. Unaware that the invaders were really deputy sheriffs, a group of armed African Americans trying to defend Moss's store fired their guns. When the blacks realized that the whites were really law enforcement officers, they stopped shooting and surrendered immediately. It was too late. One white deputy had been seriously wounded. The terrified black store owners and their friends were arrested.

The next day, curious white men from the area passed through the county jail all day long, looking over the imprisoned black men. False reports in white newspapers referred to People's Grocery as a "nest of outlaws" where drinking and gambling had taken place.[3] Moss, McDowell, and Stewart had acted in self-defense against the white lawmen, but the reports called the black men "Negro desperadoes."[4] These words inflamed the town.

Whites were incensed that one of their lawmen had been injured by blacks. The African-American community showed no signs of retaliating, yet a judge ordered officials to "shoot down on sight any Negro who appears to be making trouble."[5]

The Tennessee Rifles, a black state militia, guarded the jail. But within a few days a Shelby County judge illegally ordered the disarming of the black militia. In the middle of the night, an angry, white-masked mob, carrying Winchester rifles, forced its way into the Shelby County jail. The men dragged Moss, McDowell, and Stewart from their cells, transported them about a mile away, and shot them at close range, brutally murdering them. Another lynching, an act in which a mob murders an individual without a trial, had taken place.

Soon after hearing of Moss's death, Wells purchased a pistol and prepared to use it. She wrote, "I expected some cowardly retaliation from the lynchers. I felt that one had better die fighting against injustice than to die like a dog or rat in a trap."[6]

Wells, now part-owner and editor of the black newspaper *Free Speech*, fought back with her writing. She demanded the arrest and conviction of the lynchers. Her fiery editorial launched the first anti-lynching campaign in this country and changed the course of her life. From the tragedy of her dear friend's murder, until her own death, she devoted her time to crusading against the horrible practice of lynching. Some historians have said that her involvement in this cause was the beginning of the modern civil rights movement.[7] Wells, who had fought to keep her brothers and sisters together when their parents died and who waged a court battle to find justice on a train, had once again shown bravery.

The killers of Moss, McDowell, and Stewart were never charged. The men who had defended the black

Ida B. Wells devoted her life to protesting against lynchings such as the one pictured above.

store owners received sentences of three, eight, or fifteen years in the Tennessee state prison. White gangs took possession of People's Grocery and looted the store. Mr. Barrett bought all the remaining stock at a fraction of its cost. Wells wrote, "Thus, with the aid of the city and the county authorities and the daily papers, that white grocer had indeed put an end to his rival Negro grocer as well as to his business."[8] Later, Frederick Douglass stated, "The men lynched at Memphis were murdered because they were prosperous."[9]

In *Free Speech*, Wells encouraged African Americans to leave Memphis: "There is therefore only one thing left that we can do; save our money and leave a town which will neither protect our lives and property, nor give us a fair trial in the courts, but takes us out and murders us in cold blood when accused by white persons."[10] She even traveled to Oklahoma herself to learn firsthand what opportunities existed in the West for those African Americans who planned to leave Memphis. She reassured them that there were places where they could feel safe.

Within months, several thousand African Americans left a community that did not, and would not, protect them. They sold their homes and headed to places like Kansas, Oklahoma, and California. Some even walked the four hundred miles from Memphis to Oklahoma.

As a young woman entering her thirties, Wells

understood the economic and political strategies involved in protest.[11] As blacks left Memphis in large numbers, whites had difficulty finding servants to cook, clean, care for their children, and build their homes. Wells stayed in Memphis to protest, and she watched white store owners board up their shops and restaurants. Few blacks remained in the city to purchase the food, jewelry, pianos, clothing, and other goods whites hoped to sell.

Wells urged those who remained to keep off the streetcars, causing the City Railroad Company to suffer great financial strain. This united action by African Americans in Memphis continued to hurt the white population. Yet the white population as a whole did not realize the pain and injustice the blacks had experienced.

Throughout the spring the situation remained tense. In mid-May of 1892, a little more than two months after Moss's death, Ida B. Wells left Memphis to attend the African Methodist Episcopal (A.M.E.) Church convention in Philadelphia. Before she embarked on her journey, she wrote an editorial, which was published in the May 21 edition of *Free Speech*. It read in part: "Nobody in this section of the country believes the old threadbare lie that Negro men rape white women. If Southern white men are not careful, they will over-reach themselves and public sentiment will have a reaction. A conclusion will then be reached which will be very damaging to the moral reputation of their women."[12]

In this editorial, Wells questioned the excuses white men used to justify their lynchings of blacks: Many white men claimed black men raped white women, so, according to their logic, black men deserved to be lynched. But Wells pointed out that grocery store owners Moss, McDowell, and Stewart had not been accused of rape, yet they had been lynched. Wells later explained: "This is what opened my eyes to what lynching really was. An excuse to get rid of Negroes who were acquiring wealth and property and thus keep the race terrorized and 'keep the nigger down.' "[13]

Wells also dared to point out that some white women willingly entered into relationships with black men. The white community found this truth difficult to accept. It was common practice for a white woman to cry "rape" when family members or friends discovered that she was having a relationship with a black man. Before the accused man even had a chance to defend himself, he was lynched by a mob that took the law into its own hands.

A white newspaper reprinted Wells's editorial and referred to her as a "black scoundrel."[14] Enraged by Wells's words, many southern white men rose in protest to protect the honor of southern white women.[15] A group of influential white citizens banded together into a committee and warned the newspaper owners not to print Wells's views again. On May 27, 1892, members of the committee destroyed the presses and furnishings of *Free Speech*. Stakeouts watched trains for Wells's return. A message filtered through: If Wells returned, she would be hanged in front of the courthouse.

Later Wells remembered, "They had destroyed my paper, in which every dollar I had in the world was invested. They had made me an exile and threatened my life for hinting at the truth. I felt I owed it to myself and my race to tell the whole truth."[16]

Memphis was a dangerous place to be, and Wells believed she could be more effective in New York. She accepted a position with T. Thomas Fortune and Jerome B. Peterson, owners and editors of the *New York Age*, a prominent African-American publication. Later Wells gave them credit: "Had it not been for the courage and vision of these two men, I could never have made such headway in emblazoning the story to the world."[17]

She began to write a series on lynching, and in June 1892, the peak year of lynching in America, Wells had a seven-column, front-page article in the *New York Age*. She cited names, dates, and places to make it clear that few lynching victims had committed the crimes of which they were accused. Wells investigated every lynching she could. She visited the scenes of cruelty. She read hundreds of newspaper articles. She interviewed eyewitnesses.

Exploring 728 lynchings that had taken place within a ten-year period, she discovered that only one third of the murdered blacks had been accused of rape. Many were lynched merely because they had quarreled with a white person. She also found that not only men had been lynched, but women and children also.

Wells learned that before their deaths, lynching victims were sometimes branded with hot irons and had their eyes gouged out. Often huge crowds gathered at the carnival-like atmosphere of the lynchings. Hate was passed down from one generation to the next as onlookers, including children, cheered and later bragged that they had been at a lynching.

Wells wrote:

> The more I studied the situation, the more I was convinced that the Southerner had never gotten over his resentment that the Negro was no longer his plaything, his servant, and his source of income. The federal laws for Negro protection passed during Reconstruction times had been made a mockery by the white South where it had not secured their repeal.[18]

Her crusade against lynching drove home another important point: Even if the lynching victims' crimes had been atrocious, they were entitled to a fair trial. The Fourteenth Amendment to the United States Constitution states that every American citizen has a right to a fair trial. Lynching victims did not receive that right.

In October 1892, the year of the Moss lynching, thirty-year-old Ida B. Wells wrote, "Somebody must show that the Afro-American race is more sinned against than sinning, and it seems to have fallen upon me to do so."[19] Her crusade against lynching continued. She appealed to influential African Americans and northern whites to speak out against this injustice. The northern press ignored her story and evidence.

Frederick Douglass lent his powerful voice to her cause. Douglass, who realized that lynching was another evil that had to be challenged, praised Wells's research. "There has been no work equal to it in convincing power. I have spoken, but my word is feeble in comparison. You give us what you know and testify from actual knowledge."[20] He called Wells a "brave woman."[21]

On October 5, 1892, two hundred fifty African-American women filled New York's Lyric Hall to honor Wells for her valiant stand. Electric lights behind the podium spelled out her pen name, Iola. Programs were designed like miniature copies of *Free Speech*. Among those present were Sarah Garnet, the first black principal of an integrated school in New York and widow of the famous abolitionist Henry Highland Garnet, and Dr. Susan McKinny, a prominent African-American physician. Following a program of inspiring music and

Ida B. Wells (left) wanted to help Thomas Moss's widow and children.

speeches, Wells gave the first major speech of her career. She told the story of Thomas Moss.

Wells explained what a good person Moss was and how members of the African-American community in Memphis had respected him. She let the audience know that his wife, Betty, had been pregnant with their second child at the time Moss was murdered. They heard how Moss had begged the lynchers for his life for the sake of his wife, their child, and their unborn baby.

The pain of the Moss tragedy and the threat that she should not return home overcame Wells. She finished the powerful speech with tears streaming down her cheeks. Wells was upset with herself for crying, but the organizers of the event praised her for proving how serious lynching was.[22] The program also helped raise $500 dollars, and the first anti-lynching campaign was born. The money helped Wells continue her investigations into the causes of lynching and finance the publication of her first pamphlet, *Southern Horrors: Lynch Law in All Its Phases*.

Invitations quickly poured in from cities in the Northeast for Wells to inform America of lynchings and of white indifference toward this vile act. Armed with compelling facts, Wells reached out to all Americans.

Not everyone listened, but it was just a matter of time before Ida B. Wells's anti-lynching campaign would gain worldwide attention.

6

AN ACTIVIST AT
HOME AND
ABROAD

Less than a year after the lynching of Thomas Moss, an African-American man named Henry Smith became the victim of a particularly gruesome lynching in Paris, Texas. Local newspapers advertised the event. Schools declared a holiday to allow students to watch the accused man being burned to death. Local authorities stood by as Smith was tortured with red-hot irons and a huge fire was lit. The large mob of spectators cheered and later fought for his bones, teeth, and buttons to claim as souvenirs.

The crowd felt justified in these brutal actions because Smith had been accused of raping and murdering a five-year-old girl. But Ida B. Wells pointed out:

The man died protesting his innocence. He had no
trial, no chance to defend himself, and to this day the
world has only the word of his accusers that he
committed that horrible crime against innocent
childhood. For that reason there will always be doubts
as to his guilt. There is no doubt whatever as to the
guilt of those who murdered and tortured and burned
alive this victim of their bloodlust. They openly
admitted and gloried in their shame.[1]

The story of Henry Smith's lynching traveled
around the world. It attracted the attention of two
human rights activists, Isabelle Fyvie Mayo of Scotland
and Catherine Impey of England. Unlike many white
Americans, they wanted to know more about the lynchings in the United States and to help arouse the public
to eliminate this barbaric practice.

The two women invited Wells to come to England.
Their letter was forwarded to her while she was visiting
the home of Frederick Douglass. Douglass said to
Wells, "You go my child; you are the one to go, for you
have the story to tell."[2] She would walk in Douglass's
footsteps by speaking passionately about the evils of
lynching.

In April 1893, Wells arrived in Great Britain. The
people and press of England, Scotland, and Wales
received her warmly. Wells was well prepared for her
mission. In her suitcase she had packed newspaper
accounts, statistics, personal letters from the South,
and photographs of some of the lynching victims.
People were deeply moved as she drove home the

points that public lynchings were a crime and that these inhumane acts were happening almost daily in the United States.

Wells did not have much time for sightseeing. Instead she drafted letters, arranged meetings, and talked to the press. *The Manchester Guardian* praised Wells for being "powerful and convincing."[3]

In part because of her influence, additional chapters of the Society for the Recognition of the Brotherhood of Man were founded in England and Scotland. Each of the society's members pledged: "I, the undersigned, promise to help in securing to every member of the human family freedom, equal opportunity, and brotherly consideration."[4] They condemned lynching.

Wells had taken her crusade to Great Britain because America had not really listened to the facts about its inhumanity toward African Americans. People in the North excused and condoned lynching because they did not want to offend their southern neighbors. But Wells had confidence that British awareness of the problem of lynching in the United States could change American public opinion. She was right. The southern press, including the *Memphis Appeal-Avalanche*, the *Atlanta Constitution*, and the *Macon Telegraph*, noticed the British interest in the lynching issue. Southern journalists disliked Wells, but "they could not ignore her message."[5]

On her return voyage to the United States, Wells met fifteen charming young Englishmen. They were on their way to the 1893 World's Columbian Exposition. This world's fair, held in Chicago, would attract 27 million visitors. The English travelers were kind and attentive to Wells. She remembered, ". . . it was the first time I had met any members of the white race who saw no reason why they should not extend to me the courtesy they would have offered to any lady of their own race."[6]

On the surface, the exposition seemed a fabulous place to be, but it was a source of pain for many nonwhites. It showed the progress of Caucasians but portrayed nonwhites as childlike and barbaric. Eighty-six foreign countries were represented. Exhibits honoring the white race showcased accomplishments in manufacturing, machinery, agriculture, electricity, farming, fisheries, and forestry. A huge Ferris wheel, a recent invention, towered over all. The nonwhite races of the world were excluded from the "White City," which represented advanced civilization. The only place the nonwhite race was featured was on the Midway, represented by grass huts of a Dahomean village, sword swallowers, and belly dancers. One African-American visitor commented, "There is a lump which comes up in my throat as I pass around through all this . . . and see but little to represent us here."[7]

Wells and Douglass were determined to explain to foreign visitors why African Americans were not represented in this world showcase of progress. They were joined in this task by a prominent Chicago attorney and newspaperman, Ferdinand L. Barnett.

Wells wrote an eighty-one-page pamphlet, *The Reason Why the Colored American Is Not in the World's Columbian Exposition*, to let the world know how African Americans suffered in America. She also arranged for a series of emergency meetings with African-American women of Chicago and raised the $500 needed to print ten thousand copies. The pamphlet served as a formal protest against the exclusion of African Americans from the fair's exhibits. Wells had dreamed of seeing it published in three languages. But because of a lack of time and funds, it appeared in English with only the preface translated into French and German. In the pamphlet, Wells asked why African Americans, who had contributed so much to America's greatness, were not better represented at the fair. She went on to write of the accomplishments of African Americans and their terrible plight living in a nation of lynchings.

Exposition organizers did plan to give African Americans one day of recognition at the fair: August 25, 1893. But Wells, Douglass, and other African Americans disagreed about participating in this event. Wells believed this token day, named Colored

American Day, would dishonor African Americans. Douglass thought it was important to make the most of this small concession by fair officials. The day would go on with or without Wells.

The August heat beat down on the thousands gathered for Colored American Day. The seventy-five-year-old Douglass began his speech. A group of white hecklers who showed up to ruin the day shouted out rude remarks. The stately Douglass set down his prepared speech and glasses and looked out into the crowd. Soon his powerful voice drowned out the hecklers' cruel words. Douglass stated:

> There is no Negro problem. The problem is whether the American people have loyalty enough, honor enough, patriotism enough, to live up to their own Constitution. . . . We Negroes love our country. We fought for it. We ask only that we be treated as well as those who fought against it.[8]

Douglass spoke for more than an hour. Then several African Americans performed musical selections. A young poet named Paul Laurence Dunbar, just out of high school, recited "The Colored American," which he had written for the occasion. It was subsequently published in a book of poetry entitled *Oak and Ivy*. Dunbar would later be well known for his poem "Why the Caged Bird Sings." On that August day, these courageous African Americans took what some

Ida B. Wells considered Frederick Douglass to be the greatest leader in American history.

detractors had hoped would be a joke and turned it into a triumph.

The next morning, when Wells read about Douglass's speech, she realized her mistake and rushed to find him at the Haitian pavilion to beg his forgiveness. She acknowledged that Douglass had done more than any other to bring the concerns of the black people to the attention of white Americans. Throughout the course of the fair, thousands of white Americans came up to Douglass to shake his hand and praise his work.

Wells continued to hand out her pamphlets at the fair. She distributed the full ten thousand from the desk at the Haitian pavilion. Later she learned that some of the pamphlets ended up as far away as Russia and India.

That summer Wells also decided to move to Chicago. She began working for the *Chicago Conservator*, an African-American newspaper owned by Ferdinand L. Barnett. Both Wells and Barnett had a passion for fighting injustice, an interest they would share their entire lives. Their friendship was beginning to develop into something deeper.

In parts of Europe, Wells had seen individuals banding together in civic groups to show concern for their communities, cities, and nation. Influenced by this display of unity, Wells organized Chicago's first civic club for African-American women, which was later named in her honor.

In February 1894, after receiving an invitation from the Society for the Recognition of the Brotherhood of Man, Wells returned to England. During her six-month stay, her articles were published in the *Chicago Inter-Ocean* in a column called "Ida B. Wells Abroad." Wells earned the distinction of being the first African-American correspondent of this paper, the only white newspaper at the time to regularly condemn lynching. Wells gave credit to the *Inter-Ocean* for being "brave enough to print at length the doings, impressions, and reactions of a colored woman who was in another country pleading for justice in her own."[9]

Wells spoke to large, receptive crowds, sometimes numbering more than two thousand listeners. Applause was thunderous. She met with women's clubs and writers' groups and informed her audiences of the terrible lynchings that took place in the South. She reminded them that innocent men, women, and children were dying horrible deaths. She inspired the British to form the Anti-Lynching Committee in London to investigate and publicize the persecution of blacks in America's South. Wells hoped that the British appeal to the moral conscience of the South could stop the lynchings.[10]

During both of her trips to England, Wells treasured spending time with individuals who looked beyond the color of her skin and appreciated her thoughts and feelings.[11]

Returning to the United States in July 1894, Wells received a warm welcome at the Fleet Street A.M.E. (African Methodist Episcopal) Church in New York City. In an effort to abolish lynchings in the United States, leading ministers of England had asked American ministers to give her a chance to address their congregations at the end of Sunday services. For almost a year, she lectured throughout the northern and western states and organized more anti-lynching committees. She felt progress was being made, in part, as she wrote, "because the entire American people now feel, both North and South, that they are objects in the gaze of the civilized world and that for every lynching humanity asks that America render its account to civilization and itself."[12]

At each destination of Wells's American anti-lynching tour, special letters of welcome awaited her. They were all written by the handsome Ferdinand L. Barnett.

7

A Century Ends

n the evening of June 27, 1895, just a few weeks before her thirty-third birthday, Ida B. Wells walked down the long aisle of Chicago's crowded Bethel Church. Ferdinand Barnett found his bride radiant, dressed in a white satin gown trimmed in orange blossoms and chiffon. Wells's sisters Lily and Annie served as her bridesmaids in dresses of lemon crepe. Onlookers packed the streets, hoping to get a glimpse of the couple as they stepped into their carriage after the ceremony.

Members of the Ida B. Wells Club planned a beautiful reception. Guests extended their congratulations in a room decorated with ferns, palms, and roses.

Well-wishers included famous newspapermen and politicians. African-American papers throughout the country reported the happy news. One headline read: "Two Notable People Are Married."[1] The names of Wells-Barnett would be forever entwined, for Wells hyphenated her maiden name and her husband's name to become Ida B. Wells-Barnett.

Ferdinand Barnett's first wife had died seven years earlier. Wells became stepmother to Barnett's two sons, Ferdinand Jr. and Albert. Her new mother-in-law continued to help raise the boys, making it easier for Wells-Barnett to maintain her journalism career.

In the early days of her marriage, she served as owner, editor, publisher, and business manager of the weekly *Chicago Conservator*. Speaking engagements and club meetings also kept her busy. Her husband, thirteen years her senior, was very supportive of the work she wanted to do.

Although Wells-Barnett felt she could handle the dual roles of activist and wife, her marriage upset some of her associates. She wrote, "They seemed to feel that I had deserted the cause, and some of them censured me rather severely in their newspapers for having done so."[2]

That same year, journalist John W. Jacks, president of the Missouri Press Association, wrote a letter to the British Anti-Lynching Committee. In his letter, Jacks attacked Wells-Barnett's character and the character of

In 1895, Ida B. Wells married Ferdinand L. Barnett, a prominent
Chicago attorney and newspaperman.

all African-American women, referring to them as "prostitutes, liars, thieves, and lawbreakers."[3] The secretary of the anti-lynching organization, Florence Balgarnie, an English journalist, directed the letter to Josephine St. Pierre Ruffin, president of the Women's Era Club of Boston. Ruffin, who had admired Wells since she first heard her speak in 1892 in defense of Thomas Moss, handled the situation with dignity. She sent a copy of Jacks's vicious letter to every African-American women's club in the country and called for a meeting in Boston in July 1895.

Because it was so soon after her wedding and she was regaining strength after an exhausting anti-lynching tour, Wells-Barnett did not attend the conference. Despite her absence, the approximately one hundred conference attendees formally denounced John W. Jacks and praised "the noble and truthful advocacy of Mrs. Ida B. Wells-Barnett" and called her "Joanna of Arc."[4] At that important meeting, they created the National Federation of Afro-American Women, uniting thirty-six women's clubs in twelve states.

These women's groups had been founded in part because black women were not permitted to join white women's clubs. Created and led by African-American women, the clubs responded to the negative portrayals of African-American women in the press and encouraged self-help, education, and social reform.

The summer of 1895 marked a significant event

in the personal life of Ida B. Wells-Barnett. She was pregnant with her first child. The summer of 1895 also marked a significant event in American history: A young and very nervous African American named Booker Taliaferro Washington addressed a huge audience at the Atlanta Cotton States and International Exposition, a large fair that celebrated progress and industrial development.

As the bright Atlanta sun streamed in through the windows, Booker T. Washington delivered what was to become known as the "Atlanta Compromise" speech. "It is at the bottom of life we must begin, and not at the top," he told the group of blacks and whites who were seated in separate sections of the auditorium.[5] At one point, he held up his hand, demonstrating that although the hand had separate fingers, they could join together to form one fist. "In all things that are purely social we can be as separate as the fingers, yet one as the hand in all things essential to mutual progress."[6]

Throughout his speech, he suggested that African Americans first had to gain their economic freedom by learning employment skills and getting good jobs. Then they could fight for other kinds of freedom. "The opportunity to earn a dollar in a factory just now is worth infinitely more than the opportunity to spend a dollar in an opera house."[7] In public, Washington asked African Americans to be patient and tolerate

Booker T. Washington believed that African Americans should work to gain economic freedom before striving to achieve social equality.

segregation and discrimination for a while. In private, he donated money to African Americans who challenged unjust laws.

Many whites praised Washington's message of compromise and declared him the spokesman for all blacks. Many southern African Americans agreed with Washington's view that to keep peace between the races, it was best for African Americans to be patient.

But some African Americans felt Washington was wrong in accepting second-class citizenship for his people. Among them was Ida B. Wells-Barnett. She worried that Washington's desire to get along with the white South would further promote the mistaken notion that blacks were inferior to whites.[8] She also worried that more lynchings would take place if African Americans followed Washington's advice to postpone demanding their civil rights.[9] The debate would continue.

Six months after the famous Atlanta Compromise speech, Charles Aked Barnett was born, on March 25, 1896. The Barnetts named their firstborn after the distinguished English preacher Charles Aked, who had been one of the leaders of the anti-lynching crusade in England.

When Charles was four months old, his mother took him to Washington, D.C., to attend a historic meeting. It was the first meeting of the National Association of Colored Women (NACW). This group was formed when two black women's groups (the National Federation of Afro-American Women and the National League of Colored Women) joined together. Led by its first president, Mary Church Terrell, the NACW became the most powerful African-American women's organization in the country.

The Ida B. Wells Club of Chicago sent Wells-Barnett to the convention, where she delivered a powerful speech on reform. Other distinguished African-American participants included Frances E. W. Harper, abolitionist and suffragist; Harriet Tubman, who had been a leader of the Underground Railroad that helped slaves escape to freedom; Rosetta Douglass Sprague, daughter of Frederick Douglass; and Ellen Craft Crumb, daughter of Ellen Craft, a woman who had completed a thousand-mile escape from slavery so her children would be born on free land.

On the last day of the convention, the group elected Charles Barnett "Baby of the Association." Wells-Barnett beamed as Tubman, the organization's oldest member, presented Charles to the applauding audience.

Charles traveled with his mother in the fall of 1896 as she campaigned through Illinois for the Women's State Central Committee, a Republican political organization. At each location, the committee hired a nurse to care for Charles while his mother gave advice to women's groups on the best way to get involved in

Ida B. Wells-Barnett holds her firstborn son, Charles Aked Barnett.

political issues. Her speeches were successful, but she was disappointed to see so few black women in the audiences. "If the white women were backward in political matters, our own women were even more so," she observed.[10]

African-American rights were dealt another setback in 1896, the year of the landmark *Plessy* v. *Ferguson* U.S. Supreme Court decision. In New Orleans a few years before, Homer Adolf Plessy had refused to move from an East Louisiana Railway car reserved for whites. His case eventually ended up in the U.S. Supreme Court. The Court ruled against Plessy, stating that segregating people because of their race did not violate the United States Constitution. This decision gave federal approval to the South to impose more segregation.

After this decision, southern states and communities continued to pass more restrictive laws against African Americans. These became known as Jim Crow laws. More "Whites Only" or "Colored" signs appeared over entrances and exits of theaters, boardinghouses, and public restrooms. Eventually, Oklahoma required separate telephone booths. Atlanta had separate Bibles for black witnesses to place their hand on when swearing to tell the truth. South Carolina required separate pay windows for cotton-mill workers. Florida even required that textbooks of black and white students be stored separately. Not until 1954 would this decision be overturned in *Brown* v. *Board of Education of Topeka.*

In November 1897, the year after the *Plessy* v. *Ferguson* decision, Wells-Barnett gave birth to her second son, Herman Kohlsaat. Although Wells-Barnett enjoyed being at home, spending time with her husband and singing her sons to sleep, a tragic event inspired her to become involved once more in her crusade for justice.

In South Carolina, a mob of more than three hundred white men had killed a newly appointed black postmaster and his infant son. The postmaster's wife and four of his other children were badly wounded. Saddened by this brutal lynching, Wells-Barnett went to Washington. She took her nursing baby son, Herman, with her.

She arrived at the White House with a delegation of Illinois congressmen. They asked President William McKinley to take action in the case of the lynched black postmaster. This lynching, Wells-Barnett pointed out, was a federal matter since the postmaster had been a federal employee. Wells-Barnett urged President McKinley to support national laws to outlaw what she called "the national crime of lynching."[11] She told him, "We refuse to believe this country, so powerful to defend its citizens abroad, is unable to protect its citizens at home."[12] McKinley promised a lot, but little changed. Eventually, the eleven men who were brought to trial in a federal court in South Carolina for the postmaster's death were freed when the jury could not agree on a verdict.

During her five-week stay in Washington, Wells-Barnett urged Congress to pass a bill compensating the postmaster's widow. Her efforts were in vain. When she returned home in April 1898, the Spanish-American War was under way, and the government lost interest in Wells-Barnett's cause. She felt that even her own people lost interest in her cause: "They failed to take up the subject of organizing their forces and raising money for the purpose of sending me back to lobby for the desired results."[13]

Day after day, the white press continued to run untrue stories about black crime. In many articles, editorials, cartoons, and poems, African Americans were unjustly portrayed as liars, thieves, and uneducated fools. Race relations became even worse.

A mob of more than four hundred white men entered the black district of Wilmington, North Carolina, in November 1898. They set fire to buildings, killed and wounded many blacks, and ran hundreds more out of town. Yet President McKinley in his speech to Congress did not say one single word condemning the terrible riot. His silence disturbed the newly established Afro-American Council (AAC), whose main focus was stopping the rapid spread of southern racial injustice. Its members, including Ida B. Wells-Barnett, held an emergency meeting.

To an AAC audience composed mostly of men, Wells-Barnett delivered an impassioned speech, entitled "Mob Violence and Anarchy." She stated, "If this gathering means anything, it means that we have at last come to a point where we must do something for ourselves, and do it now. . . . We must educate the white people out of their 250 years of slave history."[14] President McKinley's lack of regard for the suffering of African Americans was another target of her speech. Some men attending the conference found her views to be too radical and called her "hotheaded."[15]

More controversy surfaced when Wells-Barnett was elected financial secretary of the AAC. The men protested: "We are compelled to regard her election to the financial secretaryship as an extremely unfortunate incident. . . . The financial secretary of the Afro-American Council should be a man—the best that can be found."[16] Their appeal to an all-male executive committee was denied; Ida B. Wells-Barnett did serve as financial secretary for one year. During that time she had to battle not only racial prejudice but also the prejudice of men of her race who resented the active role she took. Because Wells-Barnett never hesitated to take a stand, she made many enemies as well as admirers.

The following summer, in 1899, Wells-Barnett experienced another uncomfortable situation. As a member of both the NACW and the AAC, she was excited that both national conventions would be held in her hometown of Chicago during the same week. But the NACW did not ask Wells-Barnett to help plan its convention, and it did not invite her to speak.

Mary Church Terrell of the NACW explained to Wells-Barnett that some women threatened not to participate if Wells-Barnett were involved. Since Terrell depended on the Chicago leadership for the convention, she made the decision not to invite the controversial leader.

A dejected Wells-Barnett recalled the hurt in her autobiography: "It was a staggering blow and all the harder to understand because it was women whom I had started in club work, and to whom I had given all the assistance in my power, who had done this thing."[17] Even more surprising to Wells-Barnett was the fact that Terrell, whom she had met in her early days in Memphis, listened to these women: "I was still more surprised that she had obeyed the dictates of women whom she did not know against one she did know."[18]

In protest, Wells-Barnett stayed away from the NACW convention except for a short visit to relay an invitation from Jane Addams, a leading social reformer, the founder of Hull House, and, according to Wells-Barnett, "the greatest woman in the United States."[19] When Wells-Barnett did arrive, she was treated kindly by Terrell and many of the delegates.

The AAC convention later that week proved to be a better experience for Wells-Barnett. She asked for the creation of an anti-lynching bureau, and she got her request. She resigned her post as the AAC's financial secretary and became the head of the AAC's new Anti-Lynching Committee. At the convention, she attended a historic banquet at the Sherman Hotel, making her one of the first African-American women to be served dinner in a major hotel in Chicago's famous downtown Loop district.

As the nineteenth century came to a close, the nation witnessed an even greater increase in racism and discrimination toward African Americans, and these hatreds poured over into the twentieth century. An emerging African-American leader, William Edward Burghardt Du Bois, would soon state that the problem of the twentieth century was "the problem of the color line."[20] Ida B. Wells-Barnett continued her battle for justice into this new century.

8

THE STRUGGLE CONTINUES

here must always be a remedy for wrong and injustice if we only know how to find it."[1] These words were spoken by Ida B. Wells-Barnett to her husband, Ferdinand Barnett, after he shared his fears with her that the integrated school system of Chicago might soon be destroyed. It was 1900 and *The Chicago Tribune* was publishing a series of articles supporting a segregated school system for Chicago. No African-American opinions on the issues were printed. As the articles became more frequent, Ferdinand Barnett felt helpless.

Ida B. Wells-Barnett quickly took up the cause, first writing a letter to the *Tribune*. After her letter was ignored, she went directly to Robert Patterson, the newspaper's editor. When their conversation did not bring positive results, the determined Wells-Barnett asked the help of her friend Jane Addams.

Addams invited some of Chicago's most influential citizens to a gathering at Hull House. Musicians, ministers, social workers, and attorneys listened attentively as Wells-Barnett presented the case against segregated education. She told them how separate schools always meant inferior schools for African-American students. In addition, separate schools created a double tax burden for the community. She asked for the audience's support in giving African-American children "an equal chance with the children of white races."[2]

After people had heard her persuasive words, they formed a seven-member committee headed by Addams. They went to Patterson, and he stopped writing articles that advocated segregated schools.

This incident was later recorded in Wells-Barnett's autobiography: "I do not know what they did or what argument was brought to bear, but I do know that the series of articles ceased and from that day until this there has been no further effort made by the *Chicago Tribune* to separate the school children on the basis of race."[3]

In 1901, the Barnetts' first daughter was born. They named her Ida Bell Wells. Three years later, another daughter, Alfreda M., was born.

Raising their children demanded time and energy, especially as their family grew over the years, but the Barnetts also made time to be involved in the problems of the day. They shared conversations about politics and social issues. Ida could usually be seen sitting at the dining room table, sifting through stacks of newspapers and magazines. She often penned articles or revised early drafts of pamphlets. Ferdinand loved to cook and treated the family to hearty dinners usually consisting of two kinds of meat, sometimes three. Because Ida did not like doing household chores, Ferdinand hired help to do the cleaning and laundry to free her time for other responsibilities.

Ida and Ferdinand often went to literary discussions at private homes. In 1903, a Unitarian minister hosted a book discussion on the newly published *Souls of Black Folk*, written by the Harvard-educated African-American scholar W. E. B. Du Bois. In the book, Dr. Du Bois expressed his belief that both white and black Americans had to honor the traditions, culture, and values of African Americans, which he termed the "soul" of the black people in the United States.[4]

Another part of Du Bois's book attacked the public stance of Booker T. Washington, who hoped to advance the cause of blacks by keeping peace with whites. Du Bois, on the other hand, hoped to advance the cause of African Americans by fighting discrimination every step of the way.

W. E. B. Du Bois believed that African Americans should not accept segregation, but rather fight for equality among the races.

At the discussion, the Barnetts supported Du Bois's views. As some of the other participants listened to the well-informed couple, they shifted to Du Bois's point of view. Ida wrote a fan letter of sorts to Du Bois, letting him know that readers showed interest in his book. She also promised to continue discussing it at meetings. Unfortunately, their relationship would not always remain this pleasant.

In June 1905, Du Bois organized a group of African Americans into what was soon called the Niagara Movement. The Niagara Movement protested lynching, segregation of public facilities, and the denial of the black man's right to vote (women did not have the right to vote at this time). It addressed the issues of poor schools, inadequate housing, unemployment, and underemployment. It believed that the races had to cooperate to wipe out segregation. The Niagara Movement did not get the support it needed, but it did serve as the foundation for another civil rights organization that would soon emerge, the National Association for the Advancement of Colored People (NAACP), which is still active today.

The Niagara Movement's belief in cooperation between the races fell on deaf ears because many whites wanted to keep blacks "in their place." Race riots became more common. One especially brutal race riot took place in Atlanta, Georgia, in September

1906. Whites burned homes in black communities, and twelve people were killed.

More violence erupted a little less than two years later, in Springfield, Illinois, in August 1908. Angry whites torched black homes and businesses. Shouts of "Lincoln freed you, we'll show you where you belong" were heard in addition to shattering glass and gunfire.[5] At least eighty people were injured in this horrendous incident, which had taken place in the very town where the Great Emancipator, Abraham Lincoln, once lived and was now buried.

The tragedy brought whites and blacks together to discuss racial tensions and social, political, and economic conditions of African Americans in America. Three hundred blacks and whites gathered in New York on May 31 and June 1, 1909, as the National Negro Committee to form what would soon be known as the National Association for the Advancement of Colored People (NAACP).

Wells-Barnett took an active role at the New York conference. Delivering a speech titled "Lynching, Our National Crime," Wells-Barnett referred to the violent Springfield riot. "Why is mob murder permitted by a Christian nation?" she asked.[6] She requested a resolution making lynching a federal crime and reminded the participants, "Lawbreakers must be made to know that human life is sacred and that every citizen of this country is first a citizen of the United States and secondly a citizen of the state in which he belongs."[7] The proposal failed to pass. Some African-American leaders had a problem with this female crusader because she challenged the system and wanted rapid change.[8]

When it came to naming forty individuals who would spend the next year coming up with ideas for the organization, the name of Ida B. Wells-Barnett was not on the list. Some whites, upset at the turn of events, even offered to resign so there would be a place for her. The meeting adjourned. Wells-Barnett was pained and angry. Mary White Ovington, one of the founders of the NAACP, observed that Wells was "fitted for courageous work, but perhaps not fitted to accept the restraint of organization."[9]

Even though Wells-Barnett's name was eventually added to the list, she discovered that it was Du Bois who had removed her name from the original list. She felt hostile toward Du Bois, and he ignored her courageous work in the field of African-American rights in the magazine he edited, the *Crisis*, which was the official journal of the NAACP. Wells-Barnett did serve on the committee, but she never became very active in the national or local branch of the NAACP. She felt hurt by the treatment she had received.[10]

Wells-Barnett returned to the love and support of her family in Chicago. For nine years the Barnetts had lived in a two-story brick home at 3234 Rhodes Avenue. As the first African-American family on the block, they experienced discrimination. Neighbors slammed doors and stormed inside their homes whenever they saw one of the Barnetts. A gang of white boys, called the Thirty-first Street Gang, chased Charles and Herman up the front steps, shouting threats at them. A black gang formed to fight back. Although these gang members had fistfights, they did not carry and use guns, as many gangs do today.

One day while the boys taunted her children, Wells-Barnett stood in the doorway and warned the agitators that she had a pistol and was prepared to use it. No one ever saw the gun, but word got around, and the Barnett children were not bothered as much anymore. The Barnetts experienced racism firsthand, but their personal experiences were not as harsh as those of some of their fellow African Americans.

On November 11, 1909, another lynching took place, this time in Cairo, Illinois. William "Frog" James, accused of raping and murdering a white woman, was hanged, shot, and burned while he was under the protection of Sheriff Frank Davis and a deputy. After the enraged mob placed James's body on the flames of the fire they had started, they dragged the body out of the fire, cut James's head off, and stuck it on a nearby fence post.[11]

The sheriff had put up no resistance when the mob of jeering men, women, and children first came

Ida B. Wells-Barnett with her children in 1909.

for James. As a result of his inaction, the sheriff was suspended from his duties.

Ferdinand Barnett followed the story very carefully. When he learned that a hearing was scheduled to give the sheriff his job back, he knew he had to send someone to Cairo to get the facts and fight this shocking effort to reinstate the sheriff. Having complete faith in his wife's ability to handle this difficult situation, he asked her to go. She refused. She remembered that she had offended African-American men before when they accused her of trying to step in and do their jobs.

But that evening, knowing his mother very well, her oldest son, Charles, came to her bedside and whispered, "Mother, if you don't go, nobody else will."[12] The next morning, Ferdinand and the children saw Ida off at the train station. It was the first time they were happy to see her leave. They also knew that one of the special letters that she always wrote to them whenever she was away from home would arrive soon.

In Cairo, Wells-Barnett went door-to-door to gather all the facts she could about the lynching. She visited the place where the murdered woman had been found and the site of the lynching. She wrote a formal resolution that protested the reinstatement of Sheriff Davis. He should have called the governor for troops or sworn in deputies to help him, but he did not.

A famous trial lawyer and a host of supporters

accompanied Sheriff Davis into the courtroom. Ida B. Wells-Barnett arrived alone and remained alone until an African-American lawyer stopped by to extend a dinner invitation to her. Feeling sorry that she had to face this ordeal by herself, he stayed with her throughout the proceedings and provided some valuable legal advice.

Wells-Barnett presented her case in front of Governor Charles S. Deneen of Illinois. Speaking for more than four hours, she read a legal statement that Ferdinand Barnett had prepared, and then added the new facts she had uncovered. "If this man is reinstated, it will simply mean an increase of lynching in the State of Illinois and an encouragement to mob violence," she said.[13]

After her courtroom performance, white men surprised the brave crusader, tipping their hats to her and offering congratulatory handshakes. She gladly accepted their good wishes. One gentleman commented, "Whether you are a lawyer or not, you made the best speech of the day."[14]

Wells-Barnett succeeded: Sheriff Davis lost his chance at reinstatement. The court ruled that Davis did have the obligation to guarantee the life and safety of his prisoner, and he had failed to do so. The court also determined that "lynch law" could have no place in Illinois.

Praise for Wells-Barnett's role appeared in the

Chicago Defender: "If we only had a few men with the backbone of Mrs. Barnett, lynching would soon come to a halt in America."[15]

Wells-Barnett's involvement in important causes would not end there. She became more and more outspoken.

9

"That Watchdog of Human Life and Liberty"

s 1910 dawned, Ida B. Wells-Barnett continued to be "that watchdog of human life and liberty," as the *Chicago Defender* called her.[1] Now in her late forties, with sons of her own, Wells-Barnett worried about the young African-American men who had come north to build better lives. She knew it was hard for them to find good jobs and decent housing. She knew they were not allowed to rent rooms from the YMCA and the Salvation Army. She was painfully aware that they spent their free time in the places that would welcome them: the bars, pool halls, and gambling houses of Chicago's South Side.

As usual, Wells-Barnett did more than worry. She

persuaded newspaper owner Victor F. Lawson to support her idea to help homeless African Americans in Chicago and others who were in need of assistance. Not too long after, the doors of the Negro Fellowship League opened.

The center sponsored musical programs, lectures, Sunday discussions on civic responsibility, and a weekly newspaper. Young men could kick off their shoes to relax and read and play checkers. They had someone to listen to their troubles and help them locate a job or decent housing. Wells-Barnett wanted everyone coming through the doors of the Negro Fellowship League to feel a part of something special and begin to care about making life better for others, too. Although mostly men visited the center, Wells-Barnett also helped women find jobs and adjust to city life.

Never being one to sit back and delegate to others what needed to be done, Wells-Barnett worked extremely hard herself. She visited the center every day and often offered counseling. On occasion she brought a sick or troubled youth into her own home, giving him a chance to get on his feet again. Judge Jesse A. Baldwin, chief justice of the criminal court, often sent young men who appeared before him to Wells-Barnett. He knew she would provide friendship and advice. She visited young men in jail and appeared on their behalf in court. Some had been unjustly accused or received sentences that were overly harsh. She worried that the system accused many African-American men before they had a chance to defend themselves.[2]

One evening at dinner she heard that an African American named Joseph "Chicken Joe" Campbell, a convict in the Joliet Penitentiary, was locked up in solitary confinement. He had been accused of setting a fire near the warden's quarters that killed the warden's wife. For forty hours he was given only bread and water. After hearing of his plight, Wells-Barnett could not finish her meal and agonized how she might help this stranger. Eventually, she wrote newspaper articles to bring attention to his case. She also went to visit him in prison. She discovered that Campbell had no money for an attorney and had been tortured into making a confession. She encouraged her husband to get involved, even though it meant that he spent many hours away from his family and his law practice. Attorney Barnett succeeded in getting the court to change the sentence. Instead of death by hanging, Campbell would get life imprisonment.

Wells-Barnett continued to look out for others, keeping the Negro Fellowship League going even after Lawson stopped funding the center. When she served as a probation officer for three years, she contributed her entire monthly salary of $150 to the center's expenses. She worked very hard to get additional funds, but most of the middle-class African Americans chose to give their contribution to the newly formed

Urban League and the recently opened black YMCA. When the women's clubs, which she had helped to organize, supported her new competitors, she felt discouraged.[3]

While she was at the center, she made phone calls home to her children. She still found time to take them to the theater and to visit their teachers to be sure they were doing their best. Her youngest daughter, Alfreda, remembers that her mother was always busy, but she did relax when the family played whist, a card game similar to bridge. While their mother read and wrote and prepared for meetings, little Ida played the piano and Alfreda practiced for her dance recitals. The Barnett children brought laughter to their mother when they repeatedly played a funny song called "The Preacher and the Bear" on the Victrola.

Young Alfreda accompanied her mother in Chicago, marching in a parade supporting woman's suffrage—the right to vote. Alfreda wore a white streamer across the front of her white dress that said "Alpha Suffrage" as they proudly carried banners down Michigan Avenue.

The Alpha Suffrage Club for African-American women had been organized by Wells-Barnett. Members met each week in the Reading Room of the Negro Fellowship League to discuss civic and political issues. They went house to house, urging African-American women to register to vote. "The ballot is the

Ida B. Wells-Barnett poses with daughters Ida (left) and Alfreda.

right which safeguards all our rights," Wells-Barnett stated.[4]

Wells-Barnett and the other club members had to endure the jeers of men who told them to go home and take care of their babies. The women did not give up, and eventually they gained the men's support. Soon, the Second Ward of Chicago elected its first African-American councilman.

In 1913, Illinois allowed women to vote in presidential elections, making it one of the first states to support women's right to vote. Still, it was not until 1920 that the Nineteenth Amendment made woman's suffrage part of the Constitution.

Scheduled to march in the famous suffrage parade in Washington, D.C., on the eve of Woodrow Wilson's inauguration in March 1913, Wells-Barnett took a bold stand. Some southern white women threatened not to participate if black women were allowed to march alongside white women in their respective state delegations. Hearing these threats, Wells-Barnett gave an ultimatum: She would walk side by side with white members of the Illinois delegation or she would not walk at all. A compromise was reached in the Illinois ranks. Although Wells-Barnett was not seen at the beginning of the parade, she later stepped out from among the spectators and joined the parade, walking next to the white women of the state of Illinois.

After Wilson settled into his role as the twenty-eighth president of the United States, he met with Ida B. Wells-Barnett. During his campaign, Wilson had supported the advancement of African Americans. After he won the election, Wilson's administration instead encouraged separation of the races. The Post Office and the Department of the Treasury had been ordered to segregate. Partitions separated black workers' desks from white workers' desks. Blacks could not use the same cafeterias or restrooms that the white employees used.

Wilson listened to a delegation made up of Wells-Barnett and a committee of African Americans headed by William Monroe Trotter, executive secretary of the National Equal Rights League. They asked him to use his influence as president of the United States to abolish discrimination based on a person's color. Wilson said he was unaware of this discrimination but promised to check into it. Wells-Barnett reminded him that there was more going on than he ever dreamed was taking place.

Unfortunately, Wilson did not take action to stop segregation in the federal government, nor did he get back to the committee that had visited him. When the committee returned a year later, Wells-Barnett was unable to accompany the others, but she soon learned what had happened.

During the second visit, Wilson tried to convince the delegation that "segregation is not humiliating but a

benefit, and ought to be so regarded by you gentlemen."[5]
When Trotter presented the facts to Wilson that black
and white clerks had worked side by side in the federal government for more than half a century, Wilson
became angry. "Your manner offends me," he told
Trotter and refused to meet with him again.[6]

To show her support for Trotter, Wells-Barnett
invited him to speak in Chicago and stay as a guest in
her home. The Barnetts' daughter Alfreda remembered that Trotter and her mother got along
beautifully because they were both very strong in their
shared beliefs.

The Barnett children met many famous African
Americans at their dinner table. Activists A. Philip
Randolph and Chandler Owens came to get Wells-
Barnett's support before they started their magazine,
The Messenger. African-American historian Carter G.
Woodson visited just as he was forming the Association
for the Study of Negro Life and History. It became a
Thanksgiving Day tradition to invite a guest to enjoy a
home-cooked dinner with the Barnett family.

In the spring of 1917, the United States officially
entered World War I. The war and its aftermath created new conditions for African Americans. European
immigration to the United States stopped, and the war
industry drew many southern blacks to northern cities.
They worked in steel mills, stockyards, ammunition
depots, railroads, and automobile manufacturing

The Barnett family gathered in 1917, including Ferdinand's children and grandchildren from his first marriage.

plants. Women found factory jobs. Southern whites also came north to take advantage of a better life, but they brought their racial biases with them.[7]

During this time, discrimination against African Americans increased. White workers feared that the blacks would compete with them for jobs and housing. The Ku Klux Klan's white supremacist belief that whites were better than blacks spread.[8]

In May 1917 racial violence broke out in East St. Louis, Illinois, followed by more violence in July. Reports revealed that "streetcars were stopped: Negroes, without regard to race or sex, were pulled off, stoned, clubbed, and kicked. A large group of whites marched through the streets shouting that colored people should leave East St. Louis immediately and permanently."[9] White mobs chanted, "Get a nigger . . . get another" and "Burn 'em out! Burn 'em out!"[10] Fires destroyed more than two hundred houses in the city, and the flames could be seen miles away. As terrified blacks tried to flee their burning homes, whites who had lined up to observe the destruction fired shots at them. Firefighters struggled to put out one blaze while white mobs started another. Thirty-nine blacks and eight whites were killed in the gruesome riot. More than six thousand blacks were driven from the city.

Wells-Barnett traveled into the danger zone, walking through destroyed neighborhoods and talking with survivors. She traveled to Springfield, the Illinois state capital, to inform Governor Frank O. Lowden that the National Guard had stood casually by and watched as whites brutally attacked blacks.

When Wells-Barnett returned home she realized that leading African-American politicians were not happy that she had visited East St. Louis.[11] Their displeasure did not stop her. She visited the governor again and wrote several articles in the *Chicago Defender*. In part due to her efforts, the results of a congressional investigation of the riot were published and several African Americans who had been convicted were pardoned.

Very shortly after, she protested another tragic event in the nation's history. An explosive situation occurred in August 1917 in Houston, Texas. African-American soldiers, no longer willing to put up with insulting remarks from the townspeople and assaults by local police, took up arms. One hundred soldiers shot it out with police and the white citizens who had continually taunted them. When the shooting stopped, sixteen whites and four blacks lay dead.

In court-martial proceedings that did not permit appeal to the secretary of war or the president, fifty of the African-American soldiers received prison terms and twelve were quickly hanged. The twelve bodies were thrown into nameless graves.

As president of the Negro Fellowship League, Wells-Barnett protested the speed and harshness of the punishment. As she planned for a memorial service for

Ida B. Wells-Barnett wears a button supporting the martyred African-American soldiers.

the slain men, every African-American minister refused her request for the use of his church. She was angered that the same churches that had urged the young men to support their country would not protest to the government when these men were mistreated.[12]

Wells-Barnett had buttons made up that read "In Memorial Martyred Negro Soldiers," as a reminder of the inhumane treatment the African-American soldiers had received. Secret Service agents arrived, warning her that she could be arrested if she distributed any more buttons. They also accused her of criticizing the government. She stood firm: "Yes, and the government deserves to be criticized. I think it was a dastardly thing to hang those men as if they were criminals and put them in holes in the ground just as if they had been dead dogs. If it is treason for me to think and say so, then you will have to make the most of it."[13] Wells-Barnett continued distributing the buttons, and no one bothered her again for this activity.

World War I ended on November 11, 1918. More than 360,000 African Americans had served in the military to advance the cause of world freedom during the war. After the war they were still treated as second-class citizens in their own country. Competition for jobs became even more fierce, and whites felt that they, not blacks, deserved whatever jobs there were.[14]

Violence increased when African Americans began to stand up for themselves and fight back. Mobs took over cities for days. During the first year following World War I, more than seventy African Americans, several of them veterans still in military uniform, were lynched. African Americans risked being beaten in public or attacked in their homes.

When the Barnetts moved into an eight-room house originally owned by wealthy whites on Chicago's Grand Boulevard, nearby homes were bombed. Wells-Barnett responded by penning a letter to the *Chicago Tribune*. Several weeks after the bombing incident, a race war took place close to the Barnett home. During the five-day siege, beginning July 27, 1919, twenty-five blacks and fifteen whites were killed and more than five hundred people were seriously injured. Wells-Barnett again went out into the streets to investigate the events. It was dangerous, but she often risked her life to arrive at the truth.

Approximately twenty-five race riots took place in the United States during the last six months of 1919. African-American writer and political activist James Weldon Johnson named this violent time "The Red Summer."

During the turmoil, Wells-Barnett wrote about the increasing violence in Chicago, including attacks on African-American children and the beating of a black man by four whites. She implored Chicago to take action to prevent racial violence before it was too late. Not much action was taken, and violence broke out again.

Ida B. Wells-Barnett, with her husband, Ferdinand, and daughter Alfreda at 3624 Grand Boulevard Drive, Chicago, during "The Red Summer" of 1919. Looking out the window in the background is her son Herman K. Barnett.

Dealing with violence so close to home filled the crusading Wells-Barnett's days and nights. But before the year's end, another issue of racial violence that affected Ida B. Wells-Barnett took place many miles away in Elaine, Arkansas. Twelve African-American men were sentenced to die as a result of their involvement in a riot.

Wells-Barnett responded by attending protest meetings in Chicago, sending letters to influential governmental officials, and writing columns for the *Chicago Defender* in behalf of the twelve men. This complicated case would take years to resolve. Before its conclusion, it would beckon Ida B. Wells-Barnett to a place from which she had been banished many years before.

10

FINAL BATTLES

One year after "The Red Summer," the Negro Fellowship League closed its doors. Ida B. Wells-Barnett had kept the center open for ten years, but during that time had never received the support she needed. The center was behind in rent payments, and one night a worker stole furniture and equipment. Wells-Barnett had no choice.

She continued to follow the Elaine, Arkansas, case in rural Phillips County. She even worried about it as she recovered from a gallstone operation. She could not believe the initial account circulated by Arkansas authorities. They said that blacks with high-powered rifles had fired on innocent white lawmen who accidentally happened upon a union meeting. Most of Arkansas believed this version, and hysteria took over. Authorities rounded up large numbers of African Americans, labeled them "black revolutionaries," and charged them with conspiracy to murder whites and steal their land.[1] The trials ended quickly. The court issued long prison sentences to sixty-seven African Americans and condemned twelve more to death.

Because of the vigilance of organizations such as the NAACP and some courageous people, including Ida B. Wells-Barnett, new details eventually came to light. Wells-Barnett's articles in the *Chicago Defender* called attention to the fact that the Elaine riot began because the Phillips County white planters had refused to pay blacks a fair price for their cotton. This system had been in place for years. No matter how hard black farmers worked, they were always indebted to the white planters. Black farmers finally organized into the Progressive Farmers Union and protested. They met in secret for fear of retaliation. When word of the organization got out, many whites became angry. This information also appeared in the NAACP magazine, the *Crisis*. The governor of Arkansas, Charles H. Brough, was upset that the articles gave the impression that white people were responsible for the riot. He tried to stop further distribution of the *Crisis* and the *Chicago Defender*.[2]

Eyewitnesses finally came forward to prove that

Wells-Barnett took time out from her crusading work to visit with her sisters Annie and Lily, whom she helped raise after their parents died in the yellow fever epidemic.

whites had fired the first shot at that secret gathering. One eyewitness reported that after the initial incident, angry whites "shot and killed men, women, and children without regard to whether they were guilty or innocent or had any connection with the killing of anybody, or whether members of the union or not."[3]

As the NAACP attorneys took the case to the higher courts, it was revealed that the accused had been denied time to consult with their attorney, that no African Americans had served on the jury, and that torture had been used to secure confessions and testimony against the defendants in the original trial.

One of the men on death row, Al Banks, Jr., revealed: "I was frequently whipped with great severity, and was also put into an electric chair and shocked, and strangling drugs would be put to my nose to make me tell things against others, that they had killed or shot at some white people and to force me to testify against them."[4]

H. F. Smiddy, a white witness, confirmed the statements of blacks who swore they had been tortured. Metal-studded leather straps weighing seven pounds were used in the beatings. Smiddy gave specific details: "While the negroes were being whipped they were stretched out on their stomachs on the concrete floor, with four negroes [jail trusties] holding them down, one holding each hand and one holding each leg."[5] According to Smiddy, who was present during all the "interrogations," the evidence used to convict these men was forced out during these torture sessions.

While the legal battles raged, Wells-Barnett wanted to visit the condemned men. In January 1922, the fifty-nine-year-old crusader journeyed into the South after a thirty-year absence. She had been warned never to return, but she felt she had to go now.

Posing as a relative of one of the accused, she accompanied the wives, mothers, and daughters of the prisoners to the penitentiary in Little Rock, Arkansas. As one of the women whispered to the men on death row, "This is Mrs. Barnett from Chicago," they seemed happy to see her.[6] She asked the accused to write down everything they remembered, including all they had lost of their farms, crops, and animals. They sang songs about dying and forgiving their enemies.

Wells-Barnett placed her graying head close to the cell bars and spoke strong words of encouragement: "Quit talking about dying. . . . Dying is the last thing you ought to even think about, much less talk about. Pray to live and believe you are going to get out."[7] Wells-Barnett's firsthand interviews made her realize anew the terrible injustice done to these men.

Remembering how she had used the press to bring injustice to light before, she returned to Chicago and wrote a pamphlet about the Elaine riot. She raised money to print a thousand copies and had most of them distributed in Arkansas so people would know

Wells-Barnett worried day and night about the fate of these twelve men from Arkansas, who were condemned to die.

the truth.[8] In 1923 the Supreme Court ruled that the men had not had a fair trial. Eventually, all the prisoners were set free.

In the winter of 1923, one of the twelve men she had visited on death row, who had finally been released after his long nightmare in Arkansas, came calling on the Barnetts in Chicago. He thanked Wells-Barnett for what she had done for the men and, most of all, for encouraging them to think about freedom and not death.

Ida B. Wells-Barnett had lived through turbulent times. She hoped that people who had not lived through these difficult years would remember what went before them. She began her autobiography in 1928. The following words appeared in the preface:

> It is therefore for the young people who have so little of our race's history recorded that I am for the first time in my life writing about myself. . . . And so, because our youth are entitled to the facts of race history which only the participants can give, I am thus led to set forth the facts contained in this volume to them.[9]

In addition to working on her autobiography, Wells-Barnett continued to lecture and be involved in her community. She remained active in politics and encouraged other women to be involved and vote. Despite her devotion to causes, she had been unsuccessful in winning elections. In 1924 she had lost an election for the presidency of the National Association of Colored Women. Members elected Mary McLeod Bethune, who rose from poverty to become a distinguished African-American leader. Several years later, at the age of sixty-seven, Wells-Barnett lost her bid for the Illinois state senate.

At the end of the 1920s, the Great Depression hit the country. Several million people were out of work, factories cut production or closed, and many businesses went bankrupt. One in three families had no money coming in. Hungry people stood in breadlines waiting for a handout. The Depression affected the Barnetts, too. They moved from their spacious home into a small apartment. Ferdinand lost his law practice. Paid speaking engagements became rare for Ida. Her son Herman was gambling, and she worried about money.[10] Still, her family, friends, church, club meetings, correspondence, and causes kept her busy.

A few months before her sixty-ninth birthday, Wells-Barnett felt dizzy and nauseated. She soon slipped into a coma and was rushed to Chicago's Dailey Hospital. Doctors were unable to repair the damage done by uremic poisoning. Waste products normally removed by the kidneys were circulating through her blood and poisoning her. On March 25, 1931, with much of her family at her side, she died on the birthday of her eldest son, Charles. After her funeral, she was buried in Chicago's Oakwood Cemetery, in the city that she had worked so hard to make better for African Americans.

11

A Crusader's Legacy

n life, Ida B. Wells-Barnett's struggle was often a lonely one. She did not always receive the recognition she deserved. Her uncompromising attitude against injustice alienated people. But that did not deter her. This woman who had been born a slave did not back down from her beliefs.

In death, a nation who owed her so much did little to honor her. Dignitaries were not present to pay tribute, and her name did not appear on the pages of history books.

But just as she had investigated to learn the truth, many other truth seekers years later would research

Her daughter Alfreda Duster and the Reverend Carl Fugua honor the memory of Ida B. Wells-Barnett in 1963.

her life and discover the importance of her legacy. She did make an impact on the world, and slowly, in time, her memory received recognition.

In 1941, the Chicago Housing Authority opened the Ida B. Wells Housing Project.

In 1950, Chicago named her one of the outstanding women in the city's history.

In 1970, her autobiography, revealing struggle after struggle against injustice, appeared in bookstores and libraries around the country.

In 1987, the Tennessee Historic Commission placed a commemorative marker for Wells-Barnett on famous Beale Street in Memphis, a city that had once asked her never to return.

In 1990, the United States Postal Service issued a stamp honoring her as part of Black History Month, and the Public Broadcasting Service presented a tribute to her in a documentary of her life entitled *Ida B. Wells-Barnett: A Passion for Justice.*

Her story is now found in more books about the battle for civil rights.

Ida B. Wells-Barnett reminds all of us that injustice needs to be faced with courage; that sometimes we must leave the safety of our own little world and look out for individuals who have no one else to help them. Ida B. Wells-Barnett's legacy reminds us that one person willing to stand up for others can make a difference.

CHRONOLOGY

1862—Ida Bell Wells is born a slave in Holly Springs, Mississippi, on July 16.

1865—The Civil War ends.

1878—Keeps her family together after her parents die during the yellow fever epidemic.

1883—Moves to Memphis, Tennessee, to teach.

1884—Refuses to leave her seat in a first-class railroad car; wins a lawsuit against the Chesapeake, Ohio and Southwestern Railroad Company.

1887—Tennessee Supreme Court reverses the lower court's decision of 1884 and rules against Wells.

1889—Becomes a partner in the *Free Speech*.

1892—Anti-lynching crusade begins; her *Free Speech*
–1895　offices are destroyed; she is warned not to return to Memphis.

1892—Conducts anti-lynching tours in the United States and England.

1895—Marries Ferdinand Barnett, Chicago lawyer, editor, and founder of the *Chicago Conservator* on June 27; publishes a hundred-page pamphlet, *A Red Record: Tabulated Statistics and Alleged Causes of Lynching in the United States. 1892–1893–1894.*

1896—First son, Charles Aked, is born; Wells-Barnett helps found the National Association of Colored Women (NACW).

1897—Second son, Herman Kohlsaat, is born.

1898—Visits President William McKinley at the White House to seek redress in the case of a black postmaster lynched in South Carolina; elected secretary of the National Afro-American Council, a forerunner of the NAACP.

1901—Daughter Ida Bell is born.

1904—Fourth child, daughter Alfreda M., is born.

1909—Leads the successful fight against the reinstatement of Frank Davies as sheriff of Alexander County, Illinois, for failing to prevent the lynching of a black man in Cairo, Illinois.

1910—The founding of the NAACP; the Negro Fellowship League offices opened its doors.

1914—Organizes the Alpha Suffrage Club for African-American women.

1920—Closes the Negro Fellowship League.

1928—Begins to write her autobiography, *Crusade for Justice*.

1930—Runs unsuccessfully as an independent candidate for the Illinois state senate.

1931—Dies of uremia in Chicago on March 25.

CHAPTER NOTES

Chapter 1. Speaking Out Against Injustice

1. Alfreda M. Duster, ed., *Crusade for Justice: The Autobiography of Ida B. Wells* (Chicago: University of Chicago Press, 1970), p. 18.

2. Ibid., p. 19.

3. Dorothy Sterling, *Black Foremothers: Three Lives* (Old Westbury, N.Y.: Feminist Press, 1979), p. 72.

4. Duster, p. 19.

5. Ibid., p. xvii.

Chapter 2. Born a Slave

1. Norman R. Yetman, *Life Under the "Peculiar Institution,"* Selections from the Slave Narrative Collection (New York: Holt, Rinehart and Winston, 1970), p. 47.

2. Alfreda M. Duster, ed., *Crusade for Justice: The Autobiography of Ida B. Wells* (Chicago: University of Chicago Press, 1970), p. 10.

3. Paula Giddings, *When and Where I Enter: The Impact of Black Women on Race and Sex in America* (Toronto: Bantam Books, 1984), p. 21.

4. Duster, p. 9.

Chapter 3. Yellow Fever

1. Alfreda M. Duster, ed., *Crusade for Justice: The Autobiography of Ida B. Wells* (Chicago: University of Chicago Press), p. 10.

2. Ibid., p. 11.

3. Ibid., p. 16.

Chapter 4. Memphis

1. Miriam De Costa-Willis, *The Memphis Diary of Ida B. Wells: An Intimate Portrait of the Activist as a Young Woman* (Boston: Beacon Press, 1995), p. 138.

2. Ibid., p. 59.

3. Ibid., pp. 128, 135.

4. Ibid., p. 63.

5. Ibid., p. 129.

6. Ibid., p. 72.

7. Alfreda M. Duster, ed., *Crusade for Justice: The Autobiography of Ida B. Wells* (Chicago: University of Chicago Press, 1970), pp. 25–26.

8. Ibid., pp. 26–27.

9. Ibid., p. 31.

10. De Costa-Willis, p. 178.

11. Duster, p. 36.

12. Ibid., p. 37.

13. Ibid.

14. Ibid.

Chapter 5. Lynching

1. *Ida B. Wells: A Passion for Justice.* Videotape produced by William Greaves for *The American Experience* series, WGBH/Boston, WNET/New York, KCET/Los Angeles, 1990. Print materials 1989, Public Broadcasting Service.

2. Ibid.

3. Ibid.

4. Dorothy Sterling, *Black Foremothers: Three Lives* (Old Westbury, N.Y.: Feminist Press, 1979), p. 78.

5. Alfreda M. Duster. ed., *Crusade for Justice: The Autobiography of Ida B. Wells* (Chicago: University of Chicago Press, 1970), p. 51.

6. Duster, p. 62.

7. Paula Giddings, "Woman Warrior: Ida B. Wells, Crusader—Journalist," *Essence*, February 1988, p. 76.

8. Duster, pp. 51–52.

9. William S. McFeely, *Frederick Douglass* (New York: Norton, 1991), p. 361.

10. Duster, p. 52.

11. *Ida B. Wells: A Passion for Justice.*

12. Sterling, p. 82.

13. Duster, p. 64.

14. Sterling, p. 82.

15. Ibid., p. 83.

16. Duster, pp. 62–63.

17. Ibid., p. 63.

18. Ibid., pp. 70–71.

19. Mildred I. Thompson, *Ida B. Wells-Barnett: An Exploratory Study of an American Black Woman, 1893–1930* (Brooklyn: Carlson, 1990), p. 30.

20. Ibid., p. 33.
21. Sterling, p. 83.
22. Duster, p. 80.

Chapter 6. An Activist at Home and Abroad

1. Alfreda M. Duster, ed., *Crusade for Justice: The Autobiography of Ida B. Wells* (Chicago: University of Chicago Press, 1970), pp. 84–85.

2. Ibid., p. 86.

3. Jesse Carney Smith, ed., "Ida B. Wells Barnett (1862–1930)," in *Notable Black American Women* (Detroit: Gale, 1992), p. 1235.

4. Duster, p. 128.

5. Mildred I. Thompson, *Ida B. Wells-Barnett: An Exploratory Study of an American Black Woman, 1893–1930* (Brooklyn: Carlson, 1990), p. 39.

6. Duster, p. 113.

7. Elliot M. Rudwick and August Meier, "Black Man in the 'White City': Negroes and the Columbian Exposition, 1893," *Phylon: The Atlanta University Review of Race and Culture*, vol. 26, no. 4, 1965, p. 359.

8. William S. McFeely, *Frederick Douglass* (New York: Norton, 1991), p. 371.

9. Duster, p. 127.

10. "Ida B. Wells-Barnett 1862–1931," in *Contemporary Black Biography*, vol. 8 (Detroit: Gale, 1995), p. 264.

11. Duster, p. 212.

12. Thompson, p. 66.

Chapter 7. A Century Ends

1. *Ida B. Wells: A Passion for Justice.* Videotape produced by William Greaves for *The American Experience* series, WGBH/Boston, WNET/New York, KCET/Los Angeles, 1990. Print materials 1989, Public Broadcasting Service.

2. Alfreda M. Duster, ed., *Crusade for Justice: The Autobiography of Ida B. Wells* (Chicago: University of Chicago Press, 1970), p. 241.

3. Wilson Jeremiah Moses, *The Golden Age of Black Nationalism, 1850–1925* (New York: Oxford University Press, 1978), p. 115.

4. Dorothy Sterling, *Black Foremothers: Three Lives* (Old Westbury, N.Y.: Feminist Press, 1979), p. 97.

5. Henry Louis Gates Jr., ed., *Norton Anthology of African-American Literature* (New York: Norton, 1996), p. 514.

6. Ibid., p. 515.

7. Ibid., p. 516.

8. Pierre Hauser, *Milestones in Black American History, 1877–1895* (New York: Chelsea House, 1995), p. 142.

9. Jeffrey C. Stewart, *1001 Things Everyone Should Know About African-American History* (New York: Doubleday, 1996), p. 127.

10. Duster, p. 245.

11. Sterling, p. 99.

12. "Ida B. Wells-Barnett, 1862–1931," in *Contemporary Black Biography*, vol. 8 (Detroit: Gale, 1995), p. 264.

13. Duster, p. 254.

14. John Hope Franklin and August Meier, eds., *Black Leaders of the Twentieth Century* (Urbana: University of Illinois Press, 1982), p. 55.

15. Sterling, p. 102.

16. Ibid.

17. Duster, p. 258.

18. Ibid., p. 259.

19. Ibid.

20. Gates, p. 607.

Chapter 8. The Struggle Continues

1. Alfreda M. Duster, ed., *Crusade for Justice: The Autobiography of Ida B. Wells* (Chicago: University of Chicago Press), pp. 274–275.

2. Ibid., p. 277.

3. Ibid., p. 278.

4. Henry Louis Gates Jr., ed., *Norton Anthology of African-American Literature* (New York: Norton, 1996), p. 607.

5. William L. Katz, *Eyewitness: The Negro in American History* (New York: Pittman, 1967), p. 365.

6. Dorothy Sterling, *Black Foremothers: Three Lives* (Old Westbury, N.Y.: Feminist Press, 1979), p. 104.

7. Mildred I. Thompson, *Ida B. Wells-Barnett: An Exploratory Study of an American Black Woman, 1893–1930.* (Brooklyn: Carlson, 1990), p. 263.

8. *Ida B. Wells: A Passion for Justice.* Videotape produced by William Greaves for *The American Experience* series, WGBH/Boston, WNET/New York, KCET/Los Angeles, 1990. Print materials 1989, Public Broadcasting Service.

9. Mary White Ovington, *The Walls Came Tumbling Down* (New York: Schocken Books, 1947), p. 106.

10. Duster, p. 328.

11. Milton Meltzer, *The Black Americans: A History in Their Own Words* (New York: Thomas Crowell, 1964), p. 157.

12. Duster, p. 311.

13. Ibid., p. 317.

14. Ibid., p. 318.

15. Thompson, p. 117.

Chapter 9. "That Watchdog of Human Life and Liberty"

1. Mildred I. Thompson, *Ida B. Wells-Barnett: An Exploratory Study of An American Black Woman, 1893–1930* (Brooklyn: Carlson, 1990), p. 117.

2. Alfreda M. Duster, ed., *Crusade for Justice: The Autobiography of Ida B. Wells* (Chicago: University of Chicago Press, 1970), p. 337.

3. John Hope Franklin and August Meier, eds., *Black Leaders of the Twentieth Century* (Urbana: University of Illinois Press, 1982), p. 55.

4. Thompson, p. 124.

5. William L. Katz, *Eyewitness: The Negro in American History* (New York: Pitman, 1967), p. 377.

6. Ibid., p. 378.

7. Langston Hughes and Milton Meltzer, *A Pictorial History of the Negro in America* (New York: Crown, 1956), p. 268.

8. Mark E. Dudley, *Brown v. Board of Education (1954): School Desegregation* (New York: Twenty First Century Books, 1994), pp. 28–29.

9. Elliot M. Rudwick, *Race Riot in East St. Louis July 2, 1917* (Cleveland: World, 1966), p. 44.

10. Ibid., pp. 46, 48.

11. Thompson, p. 119.

12. Duster, p. 368.

13. Ibid., p. 370.

14. C. Vann Woodward, *The Strange Career of Jim Crow* (New York: Oxford University Press, 1974), pp. 113–115.

Chapter 10. Final Battles

1. Dorothy Sterling, *Black Foremothers: Three Lives* (Old Westbury, N.Y.: Feminist Press, 1979), p. 113.

2. Richard C. Cortner, *A Mob Intent on Death: The NAACP and the Arkansas Riot Cases* (Middletown, Conn.: Wesleyan University Press, 1988), pp. 23, 31–32.

3. Ibid., pp. 124–125.

4. Ibid., p. 85.

5. Ibid., p. 125.

6. Alfreda M. Duster, ed., *Crusade for Justice: The Autobiography of Ida B. Wells* (Chicago: University of Chicago Press, 1970), p. 401.

7. Ibid., p. 403.

8. Sterling, p. 114.

9. Duster, pp. 4–5.

10. Miriam DeCosta-Willis, *The Memphis Diary of Ida B. Wells: An Intimate Portrait of the Activist as a Young Woman* (Boston: Beacon Press, 1995), p. 198.

FURTHER READING

DeCosta-Willis, Miriam, ed. *The Memphis Diary of Ida B. Wells: An Intimate Portrait of the Activist as a Young Woman*. Boston: Beacon Press, 1995.

Duster, Alfreda M., ed. *Crusade for Justice: The Autobiography of Ida B. Wells*. Chicago: University of Chicago Press, 1970.

Franklin, John Hope, and August Meier, eds. *Black Leaders of the Twentieth Century*. Urbana: University of Illinois Press, 1982.

Giddings, Paula. "Black Woman Warrior." *Essence*, February 1988.

———. *When and Where I Enter: The Impact of Black Women on Race and Sex in America*. Toronto: Bantam Books, 1984.

Grant, Donald L. *The Anti-Lynching Movement, 1883–1932*. San Francisco: R and E Research Associates, 1975.

Lester, Julius. *To Be a Slave*. New York: Dial Press, 1968.

Meltzer, Milton. *The Black Americans: A History in Their Own Words*. New York: Thomas Crowell, 1964.

Smith, Jessie Carney, ed. *Notable Black American Women*. Detroit: Gale, 1992.

Sterling, Dorothy. *Black Foremothers: Three Lives*. Old Westbury, N.Y.: Feminist Press, 1979.

Stewart, Jeffrey C. *1001 Things Everyone Should Know About African-American History.* New York: Doubleday, 1996.

Thompson, Mildred I. *Ida B. Wells-Barnett: An Exploratory Study of an American Black Woman, 1893–1930.* Brooklyn: Carlson, 1990.

Townes, Emilie. "Ida B. Wells-Barnett: An Afro-American Prophet." *Christian Century,* March 15, 1989.

Videotape

Ida B. Wells: A Passion for Justice. Produced by William Greaves for *The American Experience* series, WGBH/Boston, WNET/New York, KCET/Los Angeles, 1990. Print materials 1989, Public Broadcasting Service.

Internet

http://www.lkwdpl.org/wihohio/barn-ida.htm

INDEX

HB 1381
Lisandrelli, Elaine
Ida B. Wells.

Room   Name

Lisandrelli Elaine
Ida B. Wells   1381

DATE DUE			

GAYLORD 234   PRINTED IN U. S. A.